If you have questions on the issues of modern day slavery and what you can do about it, you will want to read John Vanek's new collaborative book, *The Essential Abolitionist*. It is a fresh call to engagement in the movement that seeks to free the lives of those imprisoned, exploited, and enslaved by human trafficking. This book will not only open your eyes and bring clarity to what is happening around you but also stir your anger and show you how to get involved. This book also discusses laws, language, and solutions essential to stopping this international crime *together* in this generation. Read this book, and then sign up.

Stephen Goode
YWAM Ambassador
Justice/Compassion
Bangkok, Thailand

John has written the essential 21st century guidebook on human trafficking. Between his extensive personal expertise and that of the many guest contributors, John has built a dynamic document that will save lives. This book could be today's textbook for those with an interest in ending human trafficking and will surely educate anyone who reads it.

Kevin Willett
CEO – Public Safety Training Consultants
Redwood City, CA

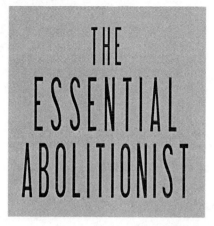

THE ESSENTIAL ABOLITIONIST

WHAT YOU NEED TO KNOW ABOUT
HUMAN TRAFFICKING
& MODERN SLAVERY

JOHN VANEK

For Dawn, my greatest collaborator.

And to Mary and Lyle,
who taught me compassion and empathy,
and the honor in serving others.

CONTENTS

PREFACE   *xiii*

CHAPTER 1
HUMAN TRAFFICKING: BASIC DEFINITIONS AND TERMS

1 – What is the Trafficking Victims Protection Act?   1
2 – How is human trafficking defined?   3
3 – How do we define and determine the use of force, fraud,
    and coercion?   5
4 – Who is a trafficker?   10
5 – What are some forms of labor trafficking?   12
6 – What are some forms of commercial sex trafficking?   14
7 – What are peonage, debt bondage, and slavery?   17
8 – Human smuggling and human trafficking: What is the
    difference?   19
9 – What does CSEC refer to?   21
10 – What is DMST?   22
11 – What is a Victim-Offender?   23
12 – What is an NGO?   25
13 – What is a VSP?   26
14 – What are CBOs and FBOs?   27
15 – What is a MANGO?   28

CHAPTER 2
MODERN SLAVERY: TRAFFICKERS AND THEIR VICTIMS

16 – How many slaves are there? (And does it really matter?)   31
17 – Why is it so difficult to determine the number of slaves?   36

18 – How do victim statistics break down for women, children, and men?   41

19 – Which is more common, labor or sex trafficking?   42

20 – Is human trafficking the most profitable type of crime?   43

21 – How much does a slave cost today?   44

22 – What is the value of a slave today?   46

23 – Which states have the most human trafficking?   48

24 – Who can become a trafficker?   51

25 – Who can become a victim?   53

26 – How do traffickers control their victims?   55

27 – What are the stages of human trafficking?   56

28 – How are runaway (and throwaway) children at risk?   58

29 – What is sex tourism, and is it trafficking?   59

CHAPTER 3
RESPONDING TO HUMAN TRAFFICKING: GENERAL CONCEPTS & RESOURCES

30 – Why should human trafficking be countered through a critical human rights approach?
Guest Contributor: Annie Isabel Fukushima, Ph.D.   61

31 – What is the 4P paradigm?   66

32 – What is a multisector response?   68

33 – What is a human trafficking task force?   70

34 – Why is collaboration so difficult to achieve?   72

35 – What is the Human Trafficking Task Force e-Guide?   75

36 – What is the National Human Trafficking Resource Center?
Guest Contributors: Sarah Jakiel & Nicole Moler   76

37 – What are the J/TIP Office and the TIP Report?
Guest Contributor: Alejandra Acevedo   84

CHAPTER 4
RESPONDING TO HUMAN TRAFFICKING: VICTIMS AND THEIR NEEDS

38 – What is a victim-centered response?   87

39 – What is a trauma-informed response?   89

40 – What are the unique needs of a trafficking victim?
Guest Contributor: Kiricka Yarbough Smith   90

41 – What legal processes may impact a trafficking survivor?
Guest Contributor: Cindy Liou   96

42 – What kinds of immigration relief are available to foreign-national survivors?
Guest Contributor: Lynette Parker   100

43 – What is the difference between a victim and a survivor?   104

44 – What is the role of a survivor in the response to human trafficking?
Guest Contributor: Shamere McKenzie   105

CHAPTER 5
RESPONDING TO HUMAN TRAFFICKING: LAW ENFORCEMENT CHALLENGES

45 – What are the challenges faced by law enforcement leaders?
Guest Contributor: Derek Marsh   109

46 – Why are human trafficking cases difficult to identify and prosecute?   116

47 – Which police units are best poised to investigate human trafficking?
Guest Contributor: Jon A. Daggy   120

48 – What strategies make a human trafficking case prosecutable?
Guest Contributor: Susan French   123

49 – What role do criminal gangs play in human trafficking?   129

50 – What is demand reduction?   131

CHAPTER 6
BE AN ABOLITIONIST: YOUR ROLE IN COMBATING HUMAN TRAFFICKING

51 – What is a modern-day abolitionist?   135

52 – How do global supply chains, human trafficking, and consumer awareness connect?
Guest Contributor: Benjamin Thomas Greer   137

53 – How do you create policy for the anti-trafficking movement that leads to real change?
Guest Contributor: Stephanie Kay Richard   140

54 – What can I do to help?   145

55 – Which traits and abilities are valuable to an abolitionist?   148

56 – "We don't have human trafficking in our community."
    How do you respond?   150
57 – How do I learn about the trafficking response in my
    community?   152
58 – How can businesses make a lasting impact on human
    trafficking?
    Guest Contributor: Mark Wexler   155
59 – How can FBOs help?
    Guest Contributor: Sandra Morgan   159
60 – What signs of trafficking can we learn to recognize?   163
61 – Which professions should receive training on human
    trafficking?   165
62 – What questions can help identify a victim?   168
63 – What types of anti-trafficking jobs exist?   170
64 – Why is self-care important for abolitionists?   172

CHAPTER 7
HUMAN TRAFFICKING: MYTHS & MISCONCEPTIONS

65 – Is the Super Bowl the "largest human trafficking
    incident" in the United States?   173
66 – Do Hollywood movies accurately portray human
    trafficking?   176
67 – Does comparing the African slave trade with modern
    slavery make sense?   178
68 – If victims are not locked and chained, why do we see
    these images?   179
69 – What are the connections between prostitution,
    pornography, and trafficking?
    Guest Contributor: Melissa Farley   180
70 – Are all sex workers victims of human trafficking?   184
71 – Are low-cost services based on labor trafficking?   186
72 – Should every case of trafficking be prosecuted as
    trafficking?   188
73 – Do high prison sentences reduce human trafficking?   189
74 – Is a "john" also a trafficker?   191
75 – Should trafficking victims ever be jailed?   193
76 – What was the impact of shutting down the Craigslist
    Adult Services section?   196

CHAPTER 8
HUMAN TRAFFICKING: FINAL QUESTIONS

77 – Who was William Wilberforce?   199
78 – What is the most heinous human trafficking crime
    I've seen?   200

ABOUT THE AUTHOR   203

ACKNOWLEDGMENTS   205

CONTRIBUTOR BIOGRAPHIES   209

RESOURCES & WEBSITES   217

ENDNOTES   221

PREFACE

It surprises many people that slavery still exists in our world and in particular, within the United States of America. "Didn't we abolish slavery with the Civil War?" people ask. No, slavery was not abolished by the Civil War. The 13th Amendment to the U.S. Constitution, ratified in 1865, abolished the legal practice of slavery, stating, "Neither slavery nor involuntary servitude ... shall exist within the United States, nor any place subject to their jurisdiction." The 13th Amendment also created a personal right: the right to be free from slavery and involuntary servitude. Yet despite the 13th Amendment and the international law and protocols outlawing slavery, today, millions of children, women, and men are enslaved or forced to work in slavery-like conditions in every corner of the world. This new form of slavery is called human trafficking and is quite different from the slavery of the past. Today, slavery operates in a very dynamic environment: Criminals continuously invent new ways to exploit their fellow human beings; victims don't always view themselves as victims; law enforcement investigators and prosecutors face new challenges; legislators pass new state and federal laws every year; and in the meantime, organizations launch new and creative response initiatives. Both the systems of enslavement and the efforts to stop it are complex and dynamic. In addition, the response to slavery entails collaborative efforts not previously demanded.

Human trafficking touches every one of us, whether we realize it or not. The food we eat, the clothes we wear, the products we purchase may involve the involuntary labor—or even slave labor—of people we never think of when we eat, get dressed, or enjoy the products touching our lives. Sex trafficking impacts not only its victims but also our communities. We have a moral imperative to protect all who are abused, exploited, or enslaved.

For a decade I've been involved in the fight against human trafficking, first with the San Jose Police Department Human Trafficking Task Force, and now as a consultant, trainer, and speaker. I've been fortunate to be involved in educating both professionals and laypersons working to stop human trafficking and assist those victimized by traffickers. When I entered this field, few people were even aware of the term *human trafficking*. Although more people today have at least heard the term, one element of my work has not changed: The same questions are asked over and over again, whether the audience consists of anti-trafficking professionals, university students, civic or faith groups, or the general public.

These questions are understandable in light of the complexity of these two distinct and intertwined subjects: human trafficking and *the response to human trafficking*. In addition, the lack of a single resource that addresses these questions furthers the confusion that prompts them.

I've written this book in order to provide a solid foundation for future discussion, collaboration, and action between people in diverse professions and civic groups. In developing this resource, I have three distinct goals:

1. **Replacing complexity with shared understanding**
   Complexity reigns supreme in both the factors that cause and allow slavery and the challenges we face in our response. Many people believe if we could just do one or two things, we could eliminate or disrupt human trafficking. (The former is a great call-to-action, but the latter is something we can actually achieve.) If we are to make a difference, we must understand this complexity and its nuances. To oversimplify human trafficking is a disservice to victims of slavery and to those who work to oppose it and assist its victims.

2. **Providing context through a wider perspective**

   Much of the information offered in public about trafficking, its victims, and how to combat trafficking is
   presented in isolation; it is a myopic view of trafficking often based upon the specific area of interest and
   background of the person or organization offering the
   information. Context is especially important when we
   examine the different ways we respond to human trafficking. If we don't examine and understand the greater
   context in which our efforts play a role, unforeseen and
   unintended consequences can be the result of our actions. Occasionally I include anecdotes from my own,
   or others', anti-trafficking experiences to help provide
   context. There is much to be learned from past successes
   and especially, failures. I offer these illustrations to foster understanding, not to pass judgment.

3. **Promoting clarity by addressing common questions and
   explaining fundamental terms**

   I've written this book to answer the most often asked
   questions about modern slavery and how we respond
   (or should be responding) to this immense human rights
   tragedy. The overarching questions presented in this
   book (or similarly-worded questions) have been asked
   thousands of times. Most of my colleagues have been
   asked these same questions too. I've written this book
   for people who seek clear and concise answers on these
   difficult and often complex questions. Where more than
   one answer or opinion exists, I have tried to offer what
   I believe is most relevant to understanding the issue
   at hand. Many other excellent resources delve deeper
   into specific topics; these sources are referenced where
   appropriate or included in the Resources & Websites
   section.

I am proud to offer this book as a multisector, collaborative
effort, featuring valuable contributions from sixteen nationally

recognized anti-trafficking experts representing a variety of roles. You may notice an occasional conflict of opinion; we don't always agree on every topic. This is a result of our different backgrounds, different anti-trafficking roles, and the resulting variety in our perspectives. The diversity of our views illustrates the dynamic environment within the response to slavery; to be an abolitionist includes listening to and understanding the perspective of others, even if we don't agree. Every contributor to *The Essential Abolitionist* is devoted to moving the response to human trafficking *forward*. Thought leadership involves examining how that response can be improved, seeking new solutions, and often challenging the status quo. These discussions inform the response to trafficking, and therefore, the contributors' content is vital.

The Essential Abolitionist can be read by jumping among the questions that interest the reader the most, but it is designed to be read from beginning to end. Each chapter builds upon the previous one, introducing terms and topics that are also touched on later in the book. Some contributor content speaks to particular audiences but should be examined by all readers for two reasons. First, all abolitionists need a basic understanding of technical topics in order to understand the complexity of the response and to improve *their* response. Second, readers who are professionally involved in the response to trafficking will find information contained in *The Essential Abolitionist* helpful in their daily responsibilities. For some readers, certain portions of this book will serve as a technical manual while other sections will increase their overall understanding of human trafficking. Though most of the topics appear framed in the context of responding to human trafficking within the United States, the principles and challenges faced within the United States are faced in all corners of the world. The lessons to be learned can be implemented everywhere. Every reader will benefit from each question addressed.

Much of this book stems from my own journey as an abolitionist. I did not begin, nor will I complete, this journey alone. I have been challenged, counseled, and inspired by many individuals. (And been forgiven for my errors or misplaced passion, too.)

JOHN VANEK

Together we have spent hundreds of hours discussing and debating every single topic examined in this book. Many trusted and valued friends and colleagues have offered their insight and expertise to both the questions addressed and the answers offered.

Ultimately, this book is about sharing what I believe to be the essential knowledge needed by the modern abolitionist. I use the term *abolitionist* to refer to anyone with an interest, passion, or professional role in opposing human trafficking. If you stand against slavery, against the exploitation of millions of people in our world today, you are an abolitionist!

These words, especially when I offer my opinions, are ultimately my own. Our understanding of human trafficking and how best to respond to slavery is dynamic; issues, and our perceived best practices, can change quickly. Except where I have cited specific sources (or the topics addressed by my guest contributors), I alone am responsible for the content, errors, or oversights. Many of my contributors and I routinely consult for private organizations, federal, state and local agencies, and law enforcement organizations. Our words do not necessarily reflect the opinions or policies of any government agency or private organization.

I hope this book will inspire you to take a stand in the fight against human trafficking, even if only by sharing what you learn from *The Essential Abolitionist.*

Freedom is the most basic of human rights, so take a moment to value your freedom. Now let's see how we can help other people achieve theirs.

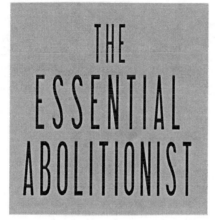

THE
ESSENTIAL
ABOLITIONIST

CHAPTER 1

Human Trafficking: Basic Definitions and Terms

If slavery is not wrong, nothing is wrong.
ABRAHAM LINCOLN

Any discussion of human trafficking or modern slavery (these terms, themselves, are used interchangeably by many individuals and organizations) must be based upon a mutual understanding of the definition of *human trafficking* along with an understanding of some of the terms commonly used by those involved in the response.

1 - What is the Trafficking Victims Protection Act?

The response to human trafficking as we recognize it and respond to it in the United States today stems from the Trafficking Victims Protection Act, which was passed by Congress and signed into law by President Clinton in October 2000.[1] The Act (or TVPA) crafted a modern and relevant definition of human trafficking, enhanced the federal laws used to prosecute traffickers, created certain protections and benefits for victims of trafficking, established certain government offices, and provided a vision for our nation's strategic response to slavery. The TVPA has since been reauthorized by Congress in 2003, 2005, 2008, and 2013. These Trafficking Victims Protection Reauthorization Acts (TVPRAs) have enhanced the laws, expanded protections for victims of trafficking, and created various programs to assist in the response to trafficking.

Through the various TVPRAs, our federal response to human trafficking has been updated and modified as we gain a better understanding of the forces that drive human trafficking and the challenges we face in our response. Many organizations actively lobby Congress for changes to the next TVPRA. Because the response to trafficking is a continual work in progress and the TVPA is, if you will, a living document, abolitionists are constantly seeking to enhance the response to trafficking based upon their understanding of the latest issues involved. Abolitionists, especially if they have a professional role, pay attention to the changes included in each reauthorization.

2 - How is human trafficking defined?

The TVPA defines human trafficking as the following.

A. *Sex Trafficking:* the recruitment, harboring, transportation, provision, or obtaining of a person for the purpose of a commercial sex act, in which the commercial sex act is induced by force, fraud, or coercion, or in which the person induced to perform such act has not attained 18 years of age; and

B. *Labor Trafficking:* the recruitment, harboring, transportation, provision, or obtaining of a person for labor or services, through the use of force, fraud, or coercion for the purpose of subjection to involuntary servitude, peonage, debt bondage, or slavery.

Several important elements of this definition need to be clearly understood. The most obvious is that there are two different categories of human trafficking, with distinct specifications. Note that both include the words "force, fraud, or coercion," which are addressed in detail later. However, there is a key distinction between these definitions. When the type of trafficking is commercial sex and the "person induced to perform such act"—the victim—is under the age of 18, no force, fraud, or coercion needs to be shown. Yet, in the specification for labor trafficking, force, fraud, or coercion needs to be shown regardless of the age of the victim.

The first category in the definition of human trafficking addresses "commercial sex acts," not sex acts in general. A commercial sex act is defined in the TVPA as "any sex act on account of which anything of value is given to or received by any person." So to be considered human trafficking, the incident must include a commercial element; something of value must be given or received. This requirement distinguishes human trafficking from, for example, rape or other forms of sexual assault where no commercial element exists. Value is often represented by money but can be satisfied by anything of recognizable value.

For now, there are three important reasons to understand these basic definitions. First, when discussing human trafficking, we must all have a mutual understanding of the definition. Second, when potential victims of human trafficking are identified, these definitions set the criteria used to classify them *as victims of trafficking*, which then allows them access to specialized benefits and reliefs available to trafficking victims by law. Finally, this definition is the standard by which individual state laws are measured, with most states using similar language in their statutory definition of human trafficking.

Two other points to clarify: The TVPA uses the term "severe forms of trafficking in persons," implying there are forms of trafficking less than "severe." This language causes confusion, but any case of human trafficking involving the use of force, fraud, or coercion is considered "severe." Also keep in mind that this definition is not a criminal statute used to prosecute traffickers. Both federal and state statutes exist which address more specific elements of the crime of human trafficking and their associated monetary and penal penalties.

In short, human trafficking is using force, fraud, or coercion to obtain commercial sex acts or other labor or services—with the exception that when the type of trafficking is commercial sex, and the victim is under 18, no force, fraud, or coercion need be shown.

3 - How do we define and determine the use of force, fraud, and coercion?

When examining any incident to determine whether it could be considered human trafficking, we must look for force, fraud, or coercion. Only one of these elements needs to be present, not all three. When examining an incident to determine whether a person should be considered a victim of trafficking, we must establish how force, fraud, or coercion was used to obtain the commercial sex act or labor or service from the victim.

When looking for force, fraud, or coercion, we must look at it from the victim's perspective, or state of mind. The degree of force needed to make one person do something they don't want to do may be far greater, or far less, for any given individual. As a result, determining the type of force, fraud, or coercion—and the extent, or degree, to which it was used—in the case of a trafficking victim is especially difficult. Investigators and prosecutors seeking proof of force, fraud, or coercion must examine the evidence in detail and will often find, for example, that fraud is difficult to distinguish from coercion. Because even professionals debate among themselves what constitutes force, fraud, or coercion, illustrating each element in more detail can be helpful.

Force is the use, or potential use, of physical power or violence. Physically assaulting or threatening to assault a victim in order to force them to perform an act of labor or commercial sex is the most common example of force. A trafficker need not actually assault the victim; simply threatening to assault the victim can constitute force. Also, violence threatened against another person can be considered force—even if the trafficker does not have the ability to actually commit the violence—so long as the victim reasonably believes they do. For example, a trafficker may threaten to harm a victim's family if the victim does not comply with the trafficker's demands. Even if the victim's family is located in another state or country and the trafficker has no realistic way to carry out the threat, if the victim *reasonably believes the threat is real,* this threat can be regarded as force (or coercion, as we will learn).

Force can also be seen as constraint if, for example, a victim is locked in a sweat shop and forced to sew clothing. But constraint does not always mean being locked in a room; a victim who is not allowed to eat if they do not perform or complete their labor is constrained from eating; often, victims of street-level commercial sex trafficking are not allowed by their pimp or trafficker to eat until they have performed a certain number of "tricks" (i.e., performed sex acts with a purchaser).

In legal terms, fraud commonly refers to misrepresenting facts through words or conduct, or by concealing or omitting facts that should have been disclosed with the intention to deceive another person. Perhaps the most common method of recruiting a slave is simply offering them a job. If a trafficker offers a job they know does not, in fact, exist, or if they lie about the working conditions and salary of a job, they are using fraud to obtain the victim's labor or services. Let's say a trafficker offers a woman a job working as a domestic servant in another country and offers to pay the transportation costs, which the woman will repay through her earnings. The trafficker promises the victim a certain salary and work conditions. However, when the victim arrives she finds she is forced to work more hours or for less pay than originally promised. The victim may feel compelled to continue to work simply because she does not have the money to return home or because she is hopeful conditions will improve. If it can be shown that the trafficker never intended to pay the victim as offered, this could constitute fraud.

Fraud can also lead to the use of force. Suppose the trafficker in the above scenario offers the same woman the same job, but the trafficker knows, in reality, no such job exists and when the woman arrives she will be forced to work in a brothel to "repay" the transportation costs. When the woman refuses to work in the brothel, violence is used (or threatened) to force the woman to work. Fraud was used to get the woman to voluntarily travel from her home to the country in which the commercial-sex exploitation occurs, and force was used to compel her to do work she did not want to do.

Traffickers also defraud victims by telling them the salary they will earn will be paid to family members, yet the earnings are never sent to the family. The trafficker is obtaining labor from the victim who works willingly, believing their family is receiving the money. In this scenario, the trafficker will have to monitor any communication between the victim and their family so the ruse will not be discovered. Despite the fact that the labor in this case is provided willingly and the victim is not constrained or threatened with force, this situation meets the definition of human trafficking.

Coercion can be a more difficult element to understand. Luckily the term is defined in the United States Code, Title 22, Chapter 78, § 7102.[2]

The term "coercion" means—

A. threats of serious harm to or physical restraint against any person;
B. any scheme, plan, or pattern intended to cause a person to believe that failure to perform an act would result in serious harm to or physical restraint against any person; or
C. the abuse or threatened abuse of the legal process.

The definition speaks to "threats of serious harm" or a "pattern intended to cause a person to believe that failure to perform an act would result in serious harm." Coercion does not require an actual act of violence; coercion is used to control a victim's state of mind, or their perceptions, and gain compliance through fear. It is also important to understand that the threatened harm can be against "any person" and not necessarily against the victim. A trafficker may threaten to harm a victim's family member, and if the victim complies with the trafficker *based upon the fear his family member may be harmed,* that equals coercion.

This example also illustrates how the terms "force" and "coercion" can both be used to describe the same activity, in this case threats of physical violence made by the trafficker. This overlap can lead to confusion, but the exact legal definition of these terms is most important to prosecutors and should not interfere with our general definition of human trafficking.

Section C of the definition of coercion refers to "the abuse or threatened abuse of the legal process." A common example of this form of coercion occurs when a foreign national victim either arrives in the United States without legal documentation or enters the United States on a valid short-term visa but then overstays the visa's timeframe (i.e., they do not leave the United States before their visa expires), and their traffickers threaten to turn them over to law enforcement or immigration authorities. The trafficker might tell the victim she will be imprisoned for being in the United States illegally. If the victim continues to perform the commercial sex acts, labor, or services, as demanded by the trafficker because of her fear of being imprisoned, she is being coerced. The supreme irony of this scenario is that the TVPA created victim protections to stop exactly this type of coercion! (These protections will be discussed in Chapter 4.)

In truth, most incidents of human trafficking involve some degree of two or even all three elements of force, fraud, or coercion. And though the TVPA does not require force, fraud, or coercion in incidents where the victim is under age 18 and involved in commercial sex, any force, fraud, or coercion used should be investigated and documented by investigators. (After receiving proper training it should be easy for investigators to articulate these criminal elements.) Mastering these terms is especially important for investigators and prosecutors since many laws have greater prison sentences for traffickers who use force, fraud, or coercion. For instance, under California law, a trafficker who exploits a minor through a commercial sex act—and whose use of force, fraud, coercion, fear, duress, or other means are not shown in court—can be sentenced to 5, 8, or 12 years in prison. However, if the investigator can articulate how force, fraud, and/

or coercion were used to compel the victim, the trafficker can receive a sentence ranging from 15 years to life!

These are just some common examples of how modern slaves are compelled by their traffickers to perform sex acts or labor. Every instance of trafficking must be closely examined on its own merits. Sometimes, when a trafficking incident is suspected, the most difficult part of the process is simply identifying the form and degree of force, fraud, or coercion involved.

4 - Who is a trafficker?

What characteristics and/or actions define the trafficker? The definition of a trafficker is broader than some may think. Looking again at the language from the TVPA, we see what actions constitute trafficking:

> The recruitment, harboring, transportation, provision, or obtaining of a person for labor or services, through the use of force, fraud, or coercion for the purpose of subjection to involuntary servitude, peonage, debt bondage, or slavery.

Any person involved in any of these steps may be considered a trafficker.

Harboring refers to sheltering a trafficking victim, and the person who harbors a trafficking victim need not be involved in the actual act of exploitation. Similarly, anyone providing supplies or support to a person who is or will be exploited is *provisioning* the victim and may be defined as a trafficker.

To illustrate the roles described above, let's examine this scenario. A man, whom we will refer to as Suspect A, operates a job placement business. A woman enters Suspect A's business looking for a job. Suspect A begins to recruit the woman, asking if she would be interested in a job as a hotel maid in another country. The job will pay $500 a week, plus room and board. The woman will repay Suspect A $1,000 for arranging the job placement. The soon-to-be victim wants the job but tells Suspect A she does not have a valid passport. Suspect A then offers to provide a counterfeit passport as long as the woman agrees to repay Suspect A an additional $500 from her earnings. The woman agrees, not realizing she is on the road to becoming a victim of human trafficking.

Suspect A actually works in concert with other criminals. Suspect A works with Suspect B, who provides (provisions) the false passport to the victim. Suspect C drives (transports) the victim from her home to the country where she will work and assists her in crossing the border using the false passport. Suspect C then delivers the victim to a house where another person, Suspect D, provides food and housing for a week (provisioning and harboring). Suspect E now arrives to pick up the victim. But Suspect E tells the victim that she will be paid only $100 a week, and she will also have to pay for her room and board, a cost of $75 per week. The victim realizes she will have to work 60 weeks to repay the $1,500 she owes Suspect A and protests. Suspect E threatens to beat the victim (force *or coercion*) if she doesn't do the job she promised to do. Suspect E also tells the victim that since she entered the country with a false passport, she can be imprisoned, and Suspect E threatens to turn her over to the police if she doesn't work (coercion). The victim feels trapped and goes to work as a maid, but in reality, she is a slave.

In this scenario, only Suspect E used force and coercion (again, *threats of violence* can constitute force or coercion), yet five traffickers exist in this example. Suspect A used the element of fraud (since Suspect A knew the salary would never be paid to the victim), but Suspects B, C, and D are all traffickers, too. As you can imagine, conducting a criminal investigation of this scenario becomes very difficult since these five traffickers are active in two different countries and because experienced traffickers operating an organization this complex would likely use false names and move the recruiting office regularly.

5 - What are some forms of labor trafficking?

The variety of ways a person can be exploited is limited only by the imagination—and the coercive power—of the trafficker. A complete listing of the types and forms of labor trafficking would be impossible to compile because vicious and inventive traffickers are constantly adapting, finding new ways to exploit their victims.

Commonly identified types include agricultural labor, such as picking or processing fruits or vegetables or tending livestock; domestic servitude, which often takes the form of a live-in maid cleaning the home; production labor, such as sewing garments in a sweat shop, mining operations, or the creation of other goods for sale; construction labor; commercial fishing; restaurant services; and hotel or motel custodial labor. Both adults and children have been exploited in all of these situations, and some forms are more prevalent in different regions of the world.

In many parts of the world, children are also exploited as child soldiers, defined as "any person below 18 years of age who is, or who has been, recruited or used by an armed force or armed group in any capacity, including but not limited to children, boys and girls, used as fighters, cooks, porters, spies, or for sexual purposes."[3] Estimates state approximately 300,000 children are combatants in about 30 conflicts worldwide. Criminal gangs, illegal organizations and terrorists groups also exploit children.

Other forms of labor trafficking regularly occur but are identified less often because they are more difficult for police or other agencies to investigate and because many people (including the victims) don't view these activities as potential areas of trafficking. These less recognized forms can include door-to-door magazine sales, which often exploit children or young adults who pretend to be raising money for school functions, and sidewalk sales of fruits and vegetables. The mentally and physically disabled have also been victimized by traffickers, forced to beg or to sell trinkets that appear to support programs for the disabled, when the money collected actually goes into the pockets of the traffickers.

To be effective, the abolitionist must be able to identify the types of labor most easily exploited in their geographical area. This recognition requires skill because the actual exploitation can often be counterintuitive. For example, agricultural fields exist in many parts of the United States, yet the conditions that foster potential labor trafficking vary greatly from region to region. In California, farm laborers can join unions; many of the state's agricultural fields are highly visible to the public; and most laborers have access to towns and cities that offer services to them, in part due to the dense population of the state. However, in Florida the state's topography and vegetation make the fields less visible to the public; and many of the fields are isolated from sizable towns and cities. A review of farm labor trafficking incidents seems to indicate more of this type of trafficking occurs in Florida than in California. (Additional and more thorough study and research on this topic is needed.) While we know that California and Florida both have a strong agricultural economy and that labor trafficking might power agricultural production, we can't assume an equal frequency of labor trafficking in both states.

Abolitionists need the ability to apply a nuanced view of all the factors that foster (or inhibit) labor exploitation. These skills, along with others, are addressed in greater detail in Chapter 6.

6 - What are some forms of commercial sex trafficking?

It bears reiterating: The variety of ways a person can be exploited is limited only by the imagination—and the coercive power—of the trafficker!

Before discussing forms of commercial sex trafficking, it is necessary to offer some context through which to examine the topic. Discussing sex trafficking can be challenging in many circles due to the language used. It can be seen as insensitive, or even derogatory or insulting. We examine some of these terms below. Finally, the location where the sex occurs is often used as a descriptor of a type of trafficking, but regardless of the location, the type of exploitation is the same. This practice can cause confusion and should be avoided. Abolitionists need to appreciate these differences, work to use the best language possible, and be patient with others who—though they may sound insensitive at times—are just as dedicated to assisting victims and prosecuting offenders.

Because all parties don't always agree on the basic definitions of trafficking, let's review the TVPA's specification for commercial sex: "any sex act on account of which anything of value is given to or received by any person."[4] This definition is pretty clear-cut, although I've found lawyers and other anti-trafficking professionals who debate what is "of value."

For a commercial sex act to become commercial sex trafficking, the sex act must be brought about by the use of force, fraud, or coercion by the trafficker. (The exception, of course, occurs when the victim is under age 18.) The most common form of commercial sex trafficking is forced prostitution; however, the terms *prostitution* and especially *prostitute* are seen by many as offensive—and not just by those who seek to assist victims of commercial sex trafficking, as we will explore below.

For now, assume the majority of commercial sex trafficking occurs as forced prostitution. Now we can examine the locations where this forced prostitution can occur and the mechanisms through which the buyers of the sex act locate and contact the person being forced into the act of prostitution.

Forced prostitution can occur in brothels, and the "john" (the colloquial term for a buyer of sex) visits the brothel where the sex act occurs. Brothels can secretly operate inside homes (i.e., residential brothels) or within a "front" business, meaning they operate within a supposedly legitimate business, such as a massage parlor. Traffickers and pimps use the Internet as a gateway to connect with johns and facilitate both "in call" (when the john goes to the location where the sex occurs) and "out call" (the seller goes to the john's location) meetings.

Forced prostitution also occurs on the street, with the john driving or walking to an area where those selling sex are known to congregate. Once the john meets the seller, the sex acts may occur in a car, hotel room, or some other location.

It is common to hear, "We have a victim of Internet trafficking," but this description gives us no clue to the form of forced prostitution. Better to say, "Our victim was forced to work in a residential brothel," or, "Her trafficker posted ads online and was forcing her to do outcall service." This helps us better understand exactly how the victim was being exploited and may give us insight into the history of the victim and her or his needs moving forward.

While forced prostitution is by far the most common form of commercial sex trafficking, traffickers can exploit their victims in other areas of the sex trade, for example, by forcing them to work in strip clubs or to make pornography videos. While these victims have been forced to engage in sex acts, their exploitation differs from forced prostitution. (See Question 69 for examples of how trafficking victims are sexually exploited other than through forced prostitution.)

As an aside, some people support the role in society of those who willingly engage in the sex trade. These *sex workers*—the term they prefer to use, as opposed to *prostitute*—often advocate for the legalization of the work they perform. Others who oppose the idea of legal prostitution see the use of the term *sex worker* as a way to normalize prostitution within society. While this debate over both legalization and the use of the term *sex worker* arises in connection to human trafficking, *The Essential Abolitionist* focuses only on forced commercial sexual exploitation and forced labor or services.

Later we will examine some specific terms abolitionists use when describing specific types of sex trafficking or its victims. Moving forward, I drop the use of "commercial" when discussing sex trafficking unless it is needed for a specific reason; when discussing sex trafficking, the commercial aspect is understood. While I've used the term "prostitution" to help explain this subject, it is best to avoid using this term because it can conflate issues. When discussing commercial sexual exploitation, "sex trafficking" is a better term to use than "prostitution."

Finally, the term "prostitute" should never be used to describe a victim of sex trafficking; they were engaged in *forced prostitution*. Even worse is the term "child prostitute," which implies the child chose to engage in prostitution. We will learn there are far better terms. If you must, say, "The victim was forced to engage in prostitution," or "The victim was a prostituted child."

The language of modern slavery is complex, and the next several questions examine other important terms.

7 - What are peonage, debt bondage, and slavery?

The TVPA definition of human trafficking refers to "peonage, debt bondage, or slavery." The subtle differences between these terms require review.

Both peonage and debt bondage refer to compelling a person to work to pay off a debt. The TVPA defines *debt bondage* as "the status or condition of a debtor arising from a pledge by the debtor of his or her personal services or of those of a person under his or her control as a security for debt."[5] The man who goes to work in a brick factory in India after receiving a loan from the factory owner exemplifies debt bondage. He agrees to repay his debt through his labor making bricks, but he may never be able to make enough bricks or work enough hours to repay the debt. Actual trafficking situations like this have led to multiple generations of one family living in an endless state of debt to the factory owner. The key to defining debt bondage is the debtor pledges to repay what he owes through his labor.

The term *peonage* has its roots in federal law dating back to shortly after the ratification of the 13th Amendment. Before peonage laws were passed in 1867 (but after passage of the 13th Amendment), it was legal to contract with former slaves to perform work. But if the conditions of work exploited the worker and the worker wished to leave, the law allowed the worker to be arrested and jailed—from where they could be rented out to work off fines and any debts! Peonage laws prevented this cycle of worker exploitation. Today, the term (and crime) of peonage is mostly relevant to federal prosecutors when choosing which criminal charges (e.g., involuntary servitude and/or peonage) to bring against a trafficker. When charging peonage, the prosecution must prove the existence of a debt between the trafficker and victim.

While the term *slavery* is used in a general sense and as a synonym for human trafficking, it has a specific definition: the outright ownership of another person. When someone is truly enslaved, they are owned just like any other piece of personal property. Africans were forcibly taken from Africa and then sold by slave traders to buyers in Europe and the Americas. Slavery—actually owning another person—still occurs, even though it is not legal in any country in the world. In an early trafficking case in California, a trafficker sold his victims to another trafficker for approximately $600. The second trafficker paid cold hard cash for human beings and then treated them as his property—slaves!

In the actual practice of responding to human trafficking, these terms are most important to the attorneys who prosecute traffickers. Depending upon how a specific law is written, the facts of the particular case, and how the prosecutor interprets the law, the prosecutor may seek to prove the victim was in a situation of debt bondage, peonage, or owned as a slave.

8 - Human smuggling and human trafficking: What is the difference?

Many people find the distinction between the terms "human smuggling" and "human trafficking" confusing, but these two activities are completely different. Think of it this way: Human smuggling violates a country's border; human trafficking violates a person's freedom. Although the two can occur in concert, the distinction is important.

In the typical scenario for human smuggling, the smuggler is paid to move another person illegally across a nation's border. There is physical movement involved, and both the smuggler and the person they are assisting are violating that nation's immigration policy and border sovereignty. Typically, once the smuggler has delivered the other person across the border, their relationship ends.

Human trafficking is much different. First, as defined by the TVPA and other protocols, human trafficking has nothing to do with a nation's borders; you can be a trafficker or a trafficking victim in your own nation or state. Second, no physical movement from one place to another is a required element of human trafficking. For example, a homeowner has a live-in maid to whom they pay a salary, and both the homeowner and the maid agree with the arrangement. However, one day the homeowner tells the maid she will no longer be paid a wage and if she tries to leave, she will be beaten. The maid is fearful because of the coercion applied by the homeowner and stays in the home. The maid was never moved from one location to another, but the conditions have changed. The maid is now being coerced into involuntary servitude. The homeowner is now a trafficker, and the maid is now a trafficking victim.

Though they are not the same, it is possible for human trafficking and human smuggling to occur at the same time. A trafficker may already be controlling a victim through force, fraud, or coercion and then smuggle the victim across a border to be exploited in another nation. Or, a smuggler may promise the soon-to-be-victim assistance crossing a border, and the person promises to pay the smuggler later through the income obtained from work. But once across the border, the smuggler turns trafficker when he or she applies force, fraud or coercion to exploit the victim through commercial sex or forced labor.

The distinction between these terms is simple. Smuggling is a border violation. Human trafficking is a human rights violation.

9 - What does CSEC refer to?

The response to human trafficking has evolved since the passage of the TVPA, and as a result, new terms have been created to more properly define specific types of trafficking or to better reflect a deeper understanding of the dynamics of trafficking and the role of organizations engaged in the response to trafficking.

Originally, CSEC stood for Commercial Sexual Exploitation of Children. This useful term defines a specific class of victims: children (i.e., under 18 years of age) who have been commercially sexually exploited. (A child who has been sexually exploited, but without the commercial element, is a victim of sexual assault or abuse.) But along the way someone proposed the excellent idea of using CSEC as a noun: Commercially Sexually Exploited Child. When discussing a victim, it is much better to say, "She is a CSEC," rather than "She was a prostituted child." Police officers writing reports about such incidents are encouraged to use this term.

10 - What is DMST?

DMST stands for Domestic Minor Sex Trafficking.

Again, this is an accurate term used to identify a specific type of trafficking. In the United States, *domestic* refers to a victim who is a U.S. citizen, as opposed to a foreign national, and *minor* to someone who is under age 18. Anti-trafficking professionals immediately understand that a case of DMST will be handled differently than, for example, a case of adult foreign-national sex trafficking because the needs of the victim and the elements of the crime needing to be proven are different. In everyday use you may hear someone say, "We are hosting a conference focusing on DMST," or "He was a victim of DMST."

11 - What is a Victim-Offender?

Another useful term, *victim-offender*, points to one of the nuances of human trafficking: A person can be a victim of human trafficking (or other crimes) while simultaneously being a criminal offender. The term effectively states the position a person may be in while reminding us that these individuals need to be treated respectfully as they simultaneously navigate two paths.

Victim-offenders can be adults or minors and can be victims of labor or sex trafficking. For example, a trafficking victim may be involved with their trafficker in criminal activities, such as drug sales or burglaries. It is not uncommon to arrest a person for a crime and to then learn they are a victim of human trafficking. Being a victim of one type of crime does not immediately absolve their individual culpability of other crimes. In this case, the person should be offered access to an advocate and informed of the rights and benefits available to a trafficking victim while also being processed through the criminal justice system as an offender. Their criminal acts will be investigated, the findings presented to a prosecutor, and ultimately prosecution may or may not follow.

The term *victim-offender* reminds both those who assist the trafficking victim and law enforcement officials that both aspects need to be professionally addressed. Though not recommended, it is certainly conceivable that a single police investigator could find themselves investigating a case in which they seek evidence to prove a person is a victim of trafficking and work with service providers to ensure the victim receives appropriate benefits—while simultaneously gathering evidence of criminal acts committed by the victim. Ideally, in this situation, two investigators will be utilized, each focusing on separate aspects of the case.

The victim-offender paradigm is just one more example of the complexity encountered when responding to a trafficking case. Getting professionals from both victim services and law

enforcement sectors to balance this complexity is difficult. It requires professionalism and compassion on the part of individuals
and an ability to adapt and change on the part of institutions—
agility that can be very difficult to achieve in real time.

12 - What is an NGO?

NGO is an acronym for Non-Governmental Organization. The term NGO is not specific to anti-trafficking organizations; it is used to denote organizations that may work with government agencies but are not, themselves, government agencies.

Early in the response to human trafficking, any and all organizations that were not federal, state, or local-government agencies were collectively called NGOs. Usually the NGO was an agency that provided services to trafficking victims. As the response to trafficking has grown and evolved, more specific terms have been promoted or created to better specify the type of work or services provided by NGOs. The terms below refer to subsets of NGOs and more accurately describe them or the work they perform. Often these terms are preferred by these organizations.

13 - What is a VSP?

VSP stands for Victim Services Provider, referring to agencies that directly assist victims of trafficking or other types of crime.

Victims of human trafficking, depending upon their particular situation, may require an extensive array of services including medical and mental health care, short-term and long-term housing, food and clothing, interpretation services, legal assistance for immigration or civil relief issues, employment assistance or educational support, repatriation, and family reunification. Sometimes a VSP may offer only one type of assistance, and a case manager coordinates all the services needed and the VSPs involved.

Chapters 3 and 4 will expand upon the needs of trafficking victims and the diverse group of specialists who typically work together to serve them.

14 - What are CBOs and FBOs?

Both Community-Based Organizations (CBOs) and Faith-Based Organizations (FBOs) may be involved in the response to trafficking. Both terms are often used by the individuals involved to describe the type of organization they work with, but these terms do not necessarily denote the type of work they do. Any of these different types of organizations can also, potentially, have dual roles. For example, a VSP could also be an FBO.

15 -What is a MANGO?

In 2012, my friend and colleague Kirsten Foot, professor of Communication at the University of Washington and dedicated abolitionist, invited me to co-author an article for a law enforcement executive journal. Our article examines the rising number of organizations entering the anti-trafficking sector that do not offer services to victims but instead focus on mobilizing individuals and agencies to fight human trafficking or advocate for an increased and enhanced response to slavery. In that article we coined the term MANGO: Mobilization / Advocacy, Non-Governmental Organization.[6]

We argue in that article that MANGOs should be viewed as a separate subset of the NGO category for several reasons. First, MANGOs are typically launched by passionate abolitionists, but sometimes the individuals involved have little direct experience responding to trafficking, serving the complex needs of victims, or investigating cases. As a result, their activities can sometimes be at odds with the established VSP and law enforcement response procedures and capabilities. This is not to say that the MANGO's intentions are not sound or their efforts not needed, only that in the established relationships between VSPs and law enforcement, the injection of a highly motivated MANGO can create friction. This is especially common during the time it takes for the MANGO to gain a firm and realistic understanding of the response to human trafficking in its current state.

Second, as a sector, MANGOs must be recognized by officials as having the potential for enormous impact and should therefore be included or at least acknowledged when discussing broader strategies and goals. MANGOs can be highly "disruptive" in that they may interrupt established patterns of response by other entities. Their impact can be positive, negative, neutral, or debatable—and the same can potentially be said of any organization from any sector involved in counter-trafficking efforts.

To illustrate, California Against Slavery (CAS) was founded by Daphne Phung, a young woman inspired by a documentary she watched about human trafficking.[7] With great passion and energy and limited funds, Daphne promoted her belief that increasing the prison sentences of convicted traffickers and making other changes to California law would reduce trafficking in California. She created partnerships and a following, eventually raising the money and staff needed to place an initiative on the ballot. The initiative was overwhelmingly approved by the voting public, making significant changes to California anti-trafficking laws. CAS mobilized an effort to advocate for change they believed in and succeeded, demonstrating the potential impact and power of a MANGO.

Some MANGOs are composed of one or two people, and others have multi-million dollar budgets, but collectively, they play an important role in combating human trafficking. MANGOs have influenced or created new policies at the local, regional, national, and international levels. They have created resources (such as housing for victims, thereby becoming VSPs, also) where none previously existed. They have created awareness and training programs in specialized sectors, including several initiatives around the world that train commercial flight attendants to recognize potential trafficking victims. Domestically, several MANGOs create and deliver educational programs for school students, or advocate for the inclusion of trafficking awareness education within school systems.

Awareness of the existence of human trafficking is the first step in identifying victims and bringing traffickers to justice. The work of MANGOs will continue to have a tremendous impact moving forward. Finally, the wide variety of accomplishments by MANGOs proves that if you have an idea and passion, you can create a role for yourself as an abolitionist.

CHAPTER 2

Modern Slavery: Traffickers and Their Victims

*I freed a thousand slaves. I could have freed
a thousand more if only they knew they were slaves.*
HARRIET TUBMAN

Human trafficking is vastly different from the traditional perception of slavery as practiced in the United States prior to 1865 and the ratification of the 13th Amendment. Traffickers, their victims, and their relationships vary greatly, adding to the complexity of modern slavery.

16 - How many slaves are there? (And does it really matter?)

The first question is difficult to answer. *Definitive statistics for the number of people enslaved worldwide, or even within the United States, do not exist.* All we have are estimates. Let's look at some of the most recent studies and the most commonly quoted estimates.

The International Labour Organization's 2012 report, *ILO Global Estimate of Forced Labour*, estimated 20.9 million people are in "forced labor globally, trafficked for labor and sexual exploitation, or held in slavery-like conditions."[1] Others offer slightly different estimates.

The most often quoted number of slaves worldwide, 27 million, first appeared in the 1999 book *Disposable People: New*

Slavery in the Global Economy by Kevin Bales,[2] a professor of Sociology, noted researcher, author, and co-founder of Free the Slaves, an NGO based in Washington, D.C. In *Disposable People,* Bales states that 27 million is his best estimate and a number he feels comfortable with, while acknowledging the existence of different estimates. Because *Disposable People* was one of the first books to focus on modern slavery and because Bales is a respected authority on the subject, this number—27 million—became the widely accepted standard. Currently, however, the Free the Slaves website posts an updated number to reflect the wide range in estimates of the enslaved, stating, "there are tens of millions of people in slavery today. Estimates are 21-36 million are enslaved."[3]

In his 2009 book, *Sex Trafficking: Inside the Business of Modern Slavery*, author Siddharth Kara estimated 28.4 million people were enslaved at the end of 2006.[4] Kara makes a poignant point, reminding us that regardless of the exact number currently enslaved, the number of slaves grows each year. Abolitionists face a problem that is growing, not receding.

When examining human trafficking within the United States, one fact is clear: No reliable estimate exists. While efforts have been made, most reports include the caveat that more research is necessary. Examining the studies that give some insight into the incidence (or rate) and prevalence (or distribution) of trafficking, we also see the difficulty in collection and analysis of this data.

Human trafficking task forces funded by the United States Department of Justice are required to report to the Human Trafficking Reporting System, developed by the Bureau of Justice Statistics, the Bureau of Justice Assistance, Northeastern University, and the Urban Institute. In 2011, Northeastern University released *Characteristics of Suspected Human Trafficking Incidents, 2008-2010*,[5] examining data from U.S. Department of Justice-funded human trafficking task forces for the 30-month period of January 2008 through June 2010. (Not all of the task forces—or their data—in operation during this period were included in this study.) Note the use of "Suspected Human

Trafficking Incidents" in the title. This report defines an incident as "any investigation into a claim of human trafficking, or any investigation of other crimes in which elements of potential human trafficking were identified." An investigation is "any effort in which members of the task force spent at least one hour investigating (e.g., collecting information, taking statements, and writing reports)."

The report cited 2,515 suspected incidents, with 389 incidents confirmed to be human trafficking. Of the suspected incidents, the vast majority (82%) was classified as sex trafficking, with over 1,200 incidents of alleged adult sex trafficking and 1,000 incidents of prostitution or sexual exploitation of a child. Eleven percent of the suspected incidents involved labor trafficking, while 7% were classified as an unknown trafficking type.

An incorrect assumption would be that less than 400 incidents of trafficking occurred nationwide during this period. In fact, this number represents only cases reported by the U.S. DOJ-funded task forces operating in a variety of locations across the country. (The actual number of task forces operating under this program at any one time has varied from a low of 16 to a high of 42. Data from these task forces is not sufficient to project national estimates of victims or criminal prosecutions.) No additional cases or suspected incidents from anywhere else in the country are included in this report. Also, not all task forces operate with the same level of robustness or have the same staffing levels, so it is likely the number of actual trafficking incidents was inaccurately reported.

Let's examine some commonly promoted "facts" about human trafficking in the United States. When the TVPA came into law in 2000, it was common to read "14,500-17,500 people are trafficked into the United States each year." Although this number was promoted by the federal government at the time, it was viewed as vague, at best, and has since been dropped from use by federal agencies. Still, it will occasionally be seen.

Another often-seen statement, "300,000 children are at risk of commercial sexual exploitation every year in the United

States," is drawn from a 2001 study, *The Commercial Sexual Exploitation of Children in the U.S., Canada and Mexico*, by Richard Estes and Neil Alan Weiner of the University of Pennsylvania, Center for the Study of Youth Policy.[6] The study (now over a decade old) is seen today as having several flaws. An excellent fact sheet produced in 2008 by the Crimes Against Children Research Center examined these flaws (along with flaws of other estimates). The fact sheet clearly states, "Please do not cite these numbers."[7]

A more recent attempt to determine the numbers of trafficking victims in the United States (again, unfortunately, examining only the commercial sexual exploitation of children) is the 2013 report, *Confronting Commercial Sexual Exploitation and Sex Trafficking of Minors in the United States*, produced by the National Academy of Sciences and supported by the U.S. Department of Justice.[8] The Findings and Conclusions section of this report states, "No reliable national estimate exists of the incidence or prevalence of commercial sexual exploitation and sex trafficking of minors in the United States."

Finally, illustrating that we have come full-circle in the realization that estimating the number of victims is very difficult, the *Federal Strategic Action Plan on Services for Victims of Human Trafficking in the United States* (2012),[9] a report produced through the joint efforts of the Department of Justice, Department of Health and Human Services, and the Department of Homeland Security, includes no estimate of the number of victims within the United States! Instead, the *Action Plan* states, "It is difficult to measure the magnitude of human trafficking," and like every other current report examining this issue, stresses the importance of creating better identification methods and the need for further research.

But *should* the number of individuals enslaved make a difference? Of course not! As long as one person is exploited, we need to work diligently to identify them, remove them from their enslavement, and bring traffickers to justice. To look at this another way, do we quote the number of sexual assault victims to justify our investigation and prosecution of rapists? Do we quote the number of domestic violence victims as motivation to protect these victims and provide them with assistance? Of course not! Instead, we understand these crimes must be investigated, the suspects prosecuted, and the victims assisted as they move forward with their lives.

If we want to focus on numbers, let's examine how many trafficking victims are being identified in our own communities, how many agencies are involved in the response, and how many police officers and victim advocates have received proper training on the response to human trafficking. For now we need only to understand that millions of people are enslaved worldwide and that trafficking can occur in any community in the United States. More important than the big numbers is the victim we are serving at the moment. When we are helping a trafficking victim, the most important number is one.

17 - Why is it so difficult to determine the number of slaves?

By their very nature, incidents of human trafficking are difficult to identify and quantify. As we explore some of the most common challenges, we will learn that some barriers to identification result from current reporting systems (or rather, lack of), while others arise from the relationship between the trafficker and victim. The victim's perception, or state of mind, can also be a factor. More complexity!

Let's begin with a simplified examination of how crime data is collected in the United States and how numerous factors influence the reliability of the data. If your home is burglarized, you phone your local police to report the break-in. An officer comes to your home, maybe collects some evidence, and writes a report. The officer titles the report, "Residential Burglary." After the officer files the report, a crime analyst at the police department reviews the report and enters the data into a computer database, including the crime type: Residential Burglary. Eventually this burglary, along with every other residential burglary reported in your city, is shared with the Federal Bureau of Investigation (FBI) through their Uniform Crime Reporting (UCR) Program. Every year the FBI calculates the total number of residential burglaries reported and publishes them in the annual report *Crime in the United States*.[10] This report includes every type of crime the FBI monitors, but its accuracy depends upon each law enforcement agency's voluntary reporting of crime into the database. In addition, each type of crime has a specific code, and if no code exists for a particular crime, then it cannot be tracked through this program.

The UCR Program only began tracking human trafficking in 2013 and created two codes: one for commercial sex acts and another for involuntary servitude. In late 2012, at a conference for the UCR Program's state representatives, the attendees learned about the new codes, human trafficking, the differences between types of trafficking (especially the difference between commercial sex and involuntary servitude), and the critical need for reporting human trafficking incidents. Attendees then shared this information with law enforcement analysts within their respective states.

Probably the single greatest reason we do not have more crime reporting data on human trafficking is the lack of awareness among law enforcement officers. Bear in mind, while the TVPA was passed in 2000, state-level anti-trafficking laws only began to appear mid-decade. It was not until 2013 that all 50 states had specific anti-trafficking laws. (State laws are not created equally; see the Polaris Project website for detailed analysis of this topic.) More importantly, very few states mandate that law enforcement officers receive specialized training on human trafficking. If officers don't know what human trafficking is, how can they be expected to properly report incidents? And if the incidents are not properly reported into the UCR Program, the data will not appear in the annual report. This is why training law enforcement personnel, including dispatchers, crime analysts, and others on the front lines, is critical. While strides are being made, it will take several years before human trafficking incidents will be properly reported into the UCR Program at a level from which to draw quality conclusions.

Reporting by law enforcement is not the only challenge; collecting data from VSPs is also difficult. Often VSPs serve victims of trafficking, but the crime is not reported to law enforcement (more on this topic later). Though the VSP has knowledge of an incident, that incident may go unreported to the police and therefore, uncounted. Also, since victims are often served by more than one VSP, victims can potentially be counted more than once. (Some VSPs who are part of a state- or federally-funded task force may have reporting protocols tied to their funding, but this data is usually only shared with researchers.) There is no single point universally recognized by VSPs for reporting human trafficking incidents.

In addition, because reporting trafficking incidents is time-consuming, this step becomes a low priority for everyone on the front lines when compared with assisting victims or investigating cases.

Another potential source of discrepancy in counting trafficking incidents, victims, arrests, and convictions occurs when convictions for other (non-trafficking) crimes are conflated with trafficking because prosecutors charging these cases can have their own perspective and interpretation of what crimes they count as trafficking. For example, let's consider what could happen if one suspect has been charged with multiple crimes stemming from one arrest. Let's say the case involves sex exploitation and the trafficker beat the victim to force her into the exploitation. A prosecutor may view this as human trafficking, as it clearly meets the definition. But instead of charging the suspect with trafficking, the prosecutor chooses to charge him with pimping, pandering, and assault. These are also appropriate criminal charges, but they differ from the charge of "human trafficking." Upon conviction of these charges, a prosecutor may say they obtained a conviction on a "case of human trafficking," not "the charge of human trafficking." Statements like these cause confusion because while the prosecutor may count this as a case of human trafficking, the convictions reported to the state's criminal database will not include a conviction on the specific charge of human trafficking; the convictions will be for pimping, pandering, and assault. In essence, the language used to describe—and count—trafficking cases is often inconsistent.

These examples of data collection obstacles within the United States pertain only to law enforcement and VSP reporting and don't even begin to address the many technical aspects of data collection, analysis, and reporting that researchers face when creating reliable reports. We must also bear in mind that these barriers to reporting and analysis exist worldwide. In many countries reporting is far less defined or nonexistent.

But what barriers might prevent a trafficking victim from reporting the incident themselves? The reasons can be complex, but there are common barriers that apply anywhere in the world.

In many cases, victims don't even realize they have been victimized. In many parts of the world, it is common to repay a debt through labor. But while forced labor is illegal, if victims don't know this is illegal, they don't report their victimization.

Some victims fear contacting law enforcement, either because of their immigration status or the risk of prosecution for their involvement in crimes even though the crimes may have been committed while under the control of the trafficker. Other times, the victim feels a connection (or even love) for their trafficker and does not want them arrested; this is certainly a risk in cases where a family member is the trafficker.

Sometimes a victim's reluctance to seek help is more deeply held. I once had a discussion with a woman who assisted trafficking victims in Asia. She had tried to assist a woman forced to work in a brothel. Though the victim could have walked out of the brothel and been assisted by this woman's NGO, the victim chose not to accept her help. As a Buddhist, the victim believed she was destined to the life she was living. To leave her life of suffering in the brothel would upset her karma, preventing a better life when she was reincarnated in the future.

Whether this is a correct interpretation of Buddhism is not for me to say. This is what the victim believed. This was her state of mind. As a result, her story as a victim who received assistance—and who became a survivor of human trafficking—will never be told. She remains among the uncounted.

The obstacles to accurate data collection are many. To summarize, these include the need for:

A. Accurate categories for all types of trafficking,
B. Awareness of trafficking types and how to spot them for front line responders and analysts,

C. Streamlined procedures that remove obstacles to reporting, and

D. Outreach to victims and potential victims to inform them of their rights and protections under the law.

Ultimately, reliable estimates must be achieved because they impact funding for the response to human trafficking and give us a clearer and more accurate assessment of the reality of trafficking in our communities, our nation, and our world.

18 - How do victim statistics break down for women, children, and men?

All we have are estimates.

In the International Labour Organization's 2012 report, *ILO Global Estimate of Forced Labour* (as a reminder, the ILO uses the term "forced labour" to include forced sexual exploitation), their findings state 55% of victims are women and girls, 45% men and boys. Seventy-four percent of victims are over age 18, while 26% are under age 18.[11] Other estimates exist, with different findings. But the ILO regularly reports their findings along with an explanation of their methodology. Since only estimates exist, the ILO estimates are as good as any other and probably better than most.

As mentioned earlier, there are no official estimates of how many trafficking victims exist in the United States, so estimates regarding victims' gender, age, etc., should also be regarded as broad estimates, at best.

19 - Which is more common, labor or sex trafficking?

Again referring to the *ILO Global Estimate of Forced Labour* (2012), the majority of victims (68%) are exploited through their labor, working in agriculture, domestic servitude, manufacturing, or construction, while significantly fewer (22%) are victims of forced sexual exploitation.[12] These percentages equal only 90%; the ILO estimates the remaining 10% consists of state-imposed forms of forced labor, such as prisons (outside the U.S.) where inmates are forced to perform work against their will. The subtlety in this ILO report demonstrates the importance of carefully examining and interpreting these and other estimates.

When trying to determine trends related to trafficking, such as who is more likely to be victimized or which types of trafficking occur more often, regional reports can provide useful information. Regional or state task forces, organizations which serve victims, or other localized research efforts often include this information. However, while useful, when examining these reports, it is important to keep in mind that identifiers of trafficking cases tend to find what they were looking for; if a specific effort is made to collect data regarding the sex trafficking in a particular area, the report will likely show a higher level of sex trafficking than labor trafficking cases.

Abolitionists need to be aware of these issues when quoting statistical data. Estimates are just estimates. As more effort is invested in identifying victims and investigating cases, the accuracy of this information will improve over time.

But victims of crime are human beings who need our help, and that is the message to focus on.

20 - Is human trafficking the most profitable type of crime?

No. Depending on the method used to analyze different global criminal activities, money laundering (which helps facilitate many different types of crime) generates the highest profits. In terms of specific transnational crime types, the United Nations Office on Drugs and Crime (UNODC) estimates the annual value of drug trafficking at $320 billion.[13]

In their 2014 report, *Profits and Poverty: The Economics of Forced Labour*, the ILO estimates the worldwide profits from all forms of forced labor (commercial sex and labor and services) are over $150 billion per year.[14]

As explained in the previous question, the ILO estimates 68% of trafficking victims worldwide are exploited via forced labor, while only 22% are victims of forced sexual exploitation. But the profits from these forms of trafficking are reversed: Nearly two-thirds of global profits ($99 billion) come from sex exploitation while $51 billion result from all other forms of forced labor.

In any case, estimating revenue and profit from illicit activities is very difficult. However, somewhere along the way this comparison became part of the conversation (and possibly, part of the justification) in the response to human trafficking.

But does it matter to the slave whether they are a victim of the second or third most profitable type of crime in the world? The discussion of money and trafficking has its place and will be examined later. But a victim of trafficking doesn't care how profitable global slavery is; they care only about their freedom.

21 - How much does a slave cost today?

This question arises in one of two contexts.

- How much does a slave cost today compared to the cost of a slave when slavery was legal in the United States, or;
- How much can a slave be purchased for today?

Slavery (the actual ownership of another person) does occur, making the question relevant, even though slavery is not legal in any country in the world.

One key to understanding modern slavery is to recognize that the cost of a slave today is far less than it was during the African slave trade, the primary historical context we have for comparison. As already explained, most of the enslaved today are victimized through force, fraud, or coercion; they are not physically owned—as possessions—in the manner slaves were owned two hundred years ago.

The methodology used to determine the cost of a slave in the United States in 1850 in terms of today's dollar varies. Free the Slaves estimates the cost of a slave in 1850 would be $40,000 today. Purchasing a slave in 1850 represented a significant financial investment, and though abhorrent, it was in the owner's best interest to protect that "investment." Free the Slaves estimates the average cost of a slave worldwide today is $90,[15] and in his excellent book, *A Crime So Monstrous*,[16] E. Benjamin Skinner describes a conversation between a seller and buyer in Haiti where a young girl is to be purchased—and then held and exploited for as long as the purchaser desires—for $50. In the same vein, when paying to engage in sex lasting less than an hour with a victim of trafficking exploited in a brothel, isn't the cost of the temporary slave merely what is paid? If the purchaser pays $25, is not the cost of that slave a mere $25?

As with other discussions, like comparing human trafficking to other types of crime, information like this needs some context. The common claim that "more slaves exist today than during the Trans-Atlantic slave trade," for example, also lacks critical context: The global population is far greater today!

22 - What is the value of a slave today?

In both the 1850's and today, the actual cost (dollars paid) for the slave and the income value (what could be earned by the owner from the slave's labor) are just two of the factors researchers use to determine a slave's value, or "return on investment." The value of a slave relates to the revenue generated from that slave or the savings accrued by not paying for the labor or services obtained from the slave.

Using the U.S. Federal minimum wage of $7.25 per hour, a garment manufacturing company that employs 50 people would pay $754,000 in wages annually. Add in the additional employer costs of social security, workers compensation insurance, etc., and an unscrupulous operator using force, fraud, or coercion to obtain that same labor could save close to a million dollars every year. Of course, there are some costs the trafficker must bear, such as acquisition of the slave and housing and feeding the slave, but these costs pale in comparison to the savings in salary cost.

Let's look at a different type of trafficking by a smaller criminal enterprise. A local street gang organizes a sex trafficking operation using the Internet to advertise "outcall" service, meaning the women will meet the john at his location. If the gang had five women in their "stable" (a term pimps and traffickers use to refer to the women under their control), and each woman had sex with four johns a day, and the johns each paid $80, the daily gross revenue would be $1,600. That's $584,000 per year tax free! Sadly, depending upon various factors in a particular community, this estimate could be conservative; a commercial sex operation with five women is not considered a large operation, and many victims are forced to engage in sex more than four times a day. Of course this business model can be scaled; if this financial model was used for a brothel instead of an online outcall service, and the gang operated four brothels, their yearly gross revenue could easily be in excess of $2,336,000 tax free.

While it may sound callous to use terms like "ROI," "business model" and "scaled" when referring to modern slavery, this vocabulary is critical to understanding the trafficker's mindset; they are in the business for money! Calculating the math of the forced sex trade in your particular community can help garner support for anti-trafficking efforts because once the revenue of local traffickers is understood, many law enforcement agencies work to seize the assets of traffickers just as they do for drug dealers.

Finally, if you had a domestic servant live in your home, but rather than pay their wages you forced them to work for you without pay, you would save tens of thousands of dollars in salary costs. You would also be guilty of human trafficking. Human trafficking is not always about making money; it can also be about saving money.

Human trafficking is an enormously profitable criminal enterprise. As more criminals understand this, trafficking will increase. Human trafficking needs to be understood as a money-driven crime. Being aware of the money made or saved is also critical when incidents of trafficking are identified since survivors of trafficking can collect back-wages from their trafficker (if cash or assets are seized). While the global estimates of revenue from forced labor and commercial sexual exploitation should be understood, the more relevant discussion is how trafficking can be profitable in your community. Understanding the hidden economy behind trafficking is especially important for the abolitionist helping their community recognize the complexities of modern slavery.

23 - Which states have the most human trafficking?

This question is difficult to answer largely due to the challenges of identifying cases and victims already discussed.

The National Human Trafficking Resource Center (NHTRC), operated by the Polaris Project in Washington, D.C., reports annually on the data they collect, primarily from calls and texts to the Center. In their 2014 report,[17] the top five states *reporting* incidents include California, Texas, Florida, New York, and Ohio. Over 61% of the calls or texts received were to report a "potential human trafficking tip." The Polaris Project website includes a hotspot map illustrating trends in reporting to the NHTRC. Clearly a lot of calls from these states come in to the NHTRC, which is the best source of data related to trafficking in the United States. And these states may, in fact, have the highest incidence of trafficking.

But an abolitionist should delve deeper. First, the top four states are among the most populous in the United States; this larger population represents more potential victims for exploitation. Also, many of these states have large immigrant communities which may be a factor in trafficking prevalence. In addition, California, Texas, Florida, and New York led the nation in the response to trafficking through the dedication of early activists along with the implementation of federally-funded human trafficking task forces beginning in 2005. These task forces are charged with several goals, including raising public awareness of trafficking and training local law enforcement to identify victims and prosecute cases. As a result, both independent reporting and the official response to trafficking in these states may be more robust than in others.

Another source of information frequently used (or rather, misused) to point out regional trends comes from Operation Cross Country, an annual, week-long enforcement action supported by the FBI, the National Center for Missing & Exploited

Children (NCMEC), as well as state and local law enforcement agencies. The goal of Operation Cross Country is to identify victims of commercial child sexual exploitation and the traffickers exploiting these children. The press release for the 2014 operation stated enforcement actions occurred in 106 cities across 54 FBI field divisions, recovering 168 children who were being victimized through prostitution. In addition, 281 pimps (traffickers) were arrested on state and federal charges.[18] These statistics reflect great work on the part of the agencies involved!

But these statistics have been quoted out of context by taking the numbers of victims identified and pimps arrested as proof that certain areas have a higher prevalence of trafficking. However, these numbers are the result of actions taken by law enforcement agencies just one week of the year and speak only to the particular regions where the operations were conducted. Important variables include the number of law enforcement officers dedicated to this operation within each city and how much time was actually devoted to the operation over the course of the week, variables not addressed that should be considered.

For example, in 2014, the FBI Oklahoma City field division reported two juvenile victims were identified and 14 pimps were arrested in an area with a population of 610,000. Meanwhile, the Philadelphia field division reported identifying no juvenile victims and arresting two pimps. The population of Philadelphia is 1.5 million. Meanwhile the Cleveland field division (Cleveland's population is 390,000) reported 16 juveniles recovered and 12 pimps arrested.

Clearly, the variables potentially impacting this operation at the field level must be considered. These include the number of officers involved, the hours devoted over the course of that particular week, the familiarity of law enforcement personnel with human trafficking, any other major crime incidents that could have interrupted operations, and the level of planning and preparation provided by lead agencies. Also, the operation focuses on only one week, leaving out enforcement actions during the remaining weeks of the year.

To take the results of this one operation and use the data to paint a larger picture only adds to the confusion about the incidence or patterns of trafficking. If we seek to bring clarity to these types of complex issues within the response to human trafficking, we must begin by acknowledging that complexity exists. Only then can we perform the difficult work of clarifying complex issues to educate and inform others.

We must accept that trafficking can occur in any state, often crosses state borders, and can impact anyone, regardless of socioeconomic status, cultural background, gender, age, ethnicity, or other quantifiable category. We must also accept that reliable data on the incidence and prevalence of trafficking on a national and global scale is decades away.

24 - Who can become a trafficker?

The typical trafficker is male, violent, linked to organized crime, and carrying a gun, right? Of course not, but that is how traffickers are usually portrayed in movies and TV, and much of the news reporting supports this popular profile.

The reality, however, is any type of person can become a trafficker. Remember, human trafficking is limited only by the imagination and coercive power of the trafficker. If you can think of a way to profit from another's exploitation and then successfully coerce them to do what you want, you can be a trafficker.

Let's look at some examples of convicted traffickers who don't fit the popular profile.

Wisconsin is never mentioned as a hotbed of trafficking, but in 2006, Jefferson Calimlim Sr. and his wife Elnora, both medical doctors, were convicted of enslaving a domestic servant for 19 years![19] Having a professional career, in this case as medical doctors, is no guarantee you are not willing to exploit another person for your own personal gain. In this case, the victim was enslaved by the Calimlim's for half of her life before being identified.

In 2009 Mabelle de la Rosa Dann, a single mother living in Walnut Creek, California, was convicted on charges of forced labor.[20] Dann, a native of Peru, exploited a woman who was also from Peru. Ties of language, background, culture, and place of birth are often used by a trafficker to recruit and control victims.

Also in 2009, a group including several women was convicted in Los Angeles of forcing young Guatemalan women into prostitution. Their methods for controlling their victims included threats by witch doctors that curses would be placed on them and their families if they attempted to escape.[21] This case illustrates that women can be traffickers, can work together, and can be just as vicious as any male trafficker. It also illustrates the powerful influence of religious or cultural beliefs.

Even victims of exploitation can become exploiters. This practice is common in sex exploitation cases when victims recruit other victims or work their way up to become assistants to the trafficker.

Anyone can be a trafficker. While a trafficker may fit the appearance and persona seen in films, he or she may also look just like me or you.

25 - Who can become a victim?

If anyone can become a trafficker, anyone can become a victim. The corollary to "human trafficking is limited only by the imagination and coercive power of the trafficker" is that becoming a victim only entails having a need the trafficker *appears* to fulfill and the inability (real or *perceived*) to overcome the force, fraud, or coercion applied.

In trafficking cases involving debt-bondage, for example, the victim is repaying a debt through their labor. Often the victim has received something of value from the trafficker. Perhaps the trafficker paid off a small debt or paid the transportation costs for the victim to travel to the place where the work will be performed, with the understanding that this debt will be repaid to the trafficker. The victim feels he owes a debt, and that may be true. But if the debt collector applies force, fraud, or coercion to keep the victim from leaving, then the debt collector becomes a human trafficker, and the debtor a victim of human trafficking.

This example illustrates why Free the Slaves co-founder and author, Kevin Bales, states the easiest way to exploit a person is to *offer them a job*.[22] People desperate for employment and without other options make good targets for traffickers.

While trafficking victims are often viewed by the public as relatively uneducated, timid, and perhaps unable to care for themselves, the opposite may be true; many victims of trafficking (both globally and domestically) have been empowered through education or by their families to seek a better life than the one available at home. In the course of this pursuit, these individuals can become vulnerable to exploitation.

Wouldn't it be easier if trafficking victims had a certain appearance or fit a specific demographic? Of course it would, but that simply isn't the case. No demographic is without risk. Young children, women, men, older adults, those mentally or physically impaired, those with little or no formal education, college students, those in the LGBTQ community—anyone can be victimized. Understanding this fact is critical for those involved in the response to trafficking or with the potential to have contact with trafficking victims.

However, the demographic patterns of verified victims indicate some populations tend to be more vulnerable to being enslaved than others. For example, we know that runaway children are at risk. Police officers who come into contact with runaways should be aware of this risk and inquire whether they have been exploited. Medical providers in regions where agricultural work is prevalent should be aware of whether trafficking occurs and if so, be mindful when coming into contact with farm workers seeking medical assistance. California law mandates police officers to attempt to identify victims of human trafficking when having contact with persons who have been deprived of their liberty, are suspected of engaging in prostitution, or are victims of domestic violence or sexual assault. These examples suggest how awareness of these trends can help abolitionists apply a level of multi-faceted critical thinking to their response efforts.

It is worth restating. Anyone can be a trafficker, and anyone can become a victim. Freeing ourselves from stereotypes will help us identify all types of victims exploited through all forms of trafficking.

26 - How do traffickers control their victims?

Trafficking can be described as a *state of mind* crime. I was first introduced to this concept by Andrew Huang, Assistant United States Attorney, who prosecuted some of the earliest trafficking cases in Northern California. Huang makes clear that the state of mind of both the victim *and trafficker* must be understood when examining trafficking cases.

Understanding the victim's state of mind reveals how coercion can become a powerful controlling force. When a trafficker controls a victim's state of mind, physical restraint becomes unnecessary. Victims most often live unrestrained—free of locks, chains, or barbed wire. In the *Dann* case previously mentioned, the victim was responsible for taking Dann's child to and from school every day. It was the victim's fears—her state of mind—that prevented her from walking away and reporting her exploitation to police.

Ascertaining the fears and beliefs of trafficking victims is critical to understanding how they have allowed themselves to be exploited when, to all appearances, they could have simply walked away.

How might the state of mind of a trafficker become apparent? In cases involving foreign nationals who have been exploited, it is not uncommon for the trafficker to explain—in defense of their actions—that the victim's life has been improved because of the opportunity provided by the trafficker!

Rather than list all the methods traffickers use to control their victims (an impossible task), it is better for abolitionists to change their perspective and realize that the methods of control are unlimited. Once again, we return to the maxim: Human trafficking is limited only by the imagination and coercive power of the trafficker.

27 - What are the stages of human trafficking?

Examining human trafficking as a phenomenon occurring in stages can help us understand victimization as a process—sometimes relatively short and simple, other times, longer and more complex. Various models (with differing numbers of stages and terms for each stage) have been advanced; however, a simple 5-stage model can help us see the entire process.

Stage 1: Recruitment

The trafficker identifies a potential victim and begins to recruit them, possibly through the offer of a job or by offering food, shelter, or affection. This step can be as simple as a pimp approaching a runaway on the street or as complex as a professionalized "recruitment service" promising to match laborers to work opportunities in a foreign country.

Stage 2: Transportation/Travel

Moving the victim from the point of recruitment to the place of exploitation may involve travel, but the travel involved need not be extensive. The pimp, for example, might simply walk the runaway to his apartment; the "recruitment" agent might arrange for travel to the country where the work will be done. (While travel is included here as one stage of victimization, travel is not required to meet the specifications of human trafficking.)

Stage 3: Exploitation

Through force, fraud, or coercion the runaway is compelled to engage in sex, or the laborer (now in a foreign country, perhaps without knowledge of the language, laws, or how to seek help) is forced to work.

Stage 4: End of Exploitation

The trafficker may release or abandon the victim, the victim may escape, or the exploitation may continue until the victim dies.

Stage 5: Reintegration and Survivorship

Important steps take place in this final stage, beyond the experience of victimization. The victim may be formally recognized as a trafficking victim and may receive assistance in returning to a life free of exploitation. Unfortunately, real life doesn't always conform to this ideal. Many victims never receive assistance, and sometimes the victim falls prey to other traffickers.

What's most valuable to take away from this or any other model is that trafficking—and the victimization of those exploited—can be a process, not a compartmentalized event that neatly begins or ends. And the circumstances that led to the potential for victimization may still be in place: the abusive parents that led the runaway to leave home or the unemployment that forced the laborer into the recruitment scheme.

It is worth considering human trafficking as a process when developing programs to assist victims or when designing interventions that can address the threat of trafficking at each stage, potentially resolving the underlying factors contributing to exploitation.

28 - How are runaway (and throwaway) children at risk?

Runaway children can be easy prey for pimps and traffickers. Life on the streets without food, shelter, safety, and affection are all conditions a trafficker can use to their advantage.

When discussing runaway children another term is sometimes heard: throwaway children. What is the difference between a runaway and a throwaway child? The runaway has, at least, been reported as a runaway to law enforcement. The throwaway child lacks someone who cares enough to simply phone 911. Throwaway children have been abandoned or rejected by their parents or family. They are viewed as disposable.

Recognize, too, children under age 18 are viewed differently than those who have reached "adulthood," though for most of us, little changed on our 18th birthday. We didn't become smarter or better decision makers overnight. We didn't immediately gain the ability to take better care of ourselves or to clearly anticipate the potential consequences of our actions. Our brains continue to develop into our mid-20s.

This issue is especially relevant for professionals working in the foster care system or other areas serving children because service provision can drastically change upon the child's 18th birthday, and age is a factor in how institutions classify and serve victims.

29 - What is sex tourism, and is it trafficking?

When hearing the phrase *sex tourism*, what immediately comes to mind? Usually we envision a white male, probably middle-aged or older, who travels to Asia to engage in sex with children, possibly very young children. While this is sex tourism, it is only the stereotypical image of sex tourism.

We need to adopt a broader definition of sex tourism, one that includes going anywhere to engage in commercial sex with a person whether female or male, of any age.

Traveling away from home reduces the likelihood of discovery, arrest, and being publically exposed and thus removes impediments to paying for sex. And a john who travels to any location to engage in *lawful* commercial sex is still involved in sex tourism; it just isn't *illegal* sex tourism.

While we read about major sporting events and their link to trafficking, other circumstances can just as easily provide the conditions needed for commercial sex, conditions that increase demand—and thereby, supply. Any circumstance that brings a large number of men to an area for a short duration of time, such as conventions or sporting events, *may* provide the opportunity for traffickers and pimps to exploit the demand for sex by providing the supply: victims of human trafficking. As reported in the Monterey County Weekly in 2011, events such as the ATT Pro-Am and the Concours d'Elegance car show, both of which occur in Pebble Beach, California, have the potential to create the demand and hence, the opportunity for traffickers to provide the "supply" for commercial sex.[23] Trafficking can potentially increase during these and similar types of events.

Some advertisers even suggest the opportunities available once away from home. Euphemisms like, "What happens in Vegas stays in Vegas," may provide some tacit level of approval, allowing the purchaser of sex to rationalize their activity.

CHAPTER 2

Sex tourism should be defined for what it is: an easier opportunity to engage in commercial sex with someone who is likely forced to do so. The term should be used to describe any activity of this nature.

CHAPTER 3

Responding to Human Trafficking: General Concepts & Resources

*In the long history of humankind... those who learned
to collaborate and improvise most effectively have prevailed.*
CHARLES DARWIN

With a better understanding of how to identify trafficking and
how traffickers exploit victims, we shift our attention to responding to the problem. Understanding certain fundamental concepts
allows us to more closely examine specific challenges faced by
VSPs and law enforcement.

30 - Why should human trafficking be countered through a critical human rights approach?

Guest Contributor: Annie Isabel Fukushima, Ph.D
*Dr. Annie Isabel Fukushima is an Assistant Professor in Eth-
nic Studies and Social Work at the University of Utah. Prior to
joining the faculty of University of Utah, she was an Andrew W.
Mellon Postdoctoral Fellow at Rutgers.*

What are human rights? Human rights are commonly framed
in three ways: 1) human rights are universal where all humans
are entitled to rights because they belong to the human race, 2)

human rights are culturally relative, and 3) human rights are historically situated and contingent on political and social ideologies and practices. Human rights are best understood through the example of slavery. The belief that no human shall be held in slavery or servitude is a common belief in the twenty-first century. However, during the Antebellum Period in the U.S. (pre-1865), slavery was commonly practiced and even rationalized. Slaves were not perceived of as human, but rather, property. The corrective action of the state was to abolish slavery—shifting the paradigm regarding who was entitled to rights. The antithesis to slavery is oftentimes believed to be freedom. A universal perception of human rights is freedom. Therefore, it is seemingly common sense to believe that human trafficking and slave-like practices are human rights violations.

However, in the history of the development of policy and practices regarding human trafficking in the twentieth and twenty-first centuries, there is a tension regarding human trafficking as a human rights concern and priority. In fact, human trafficking is commonly perceived of and responded to as a crime. To relegate human trafficking to the prosecutorial systems as a crime decenters the needs and experiences of those who survive trafficking. This problematically leads to privileging in the anti-trafficking movement only certain stories: when the victim is a child or a woman, one whose narrative is perfect and non-contradictory. I will next briefly historically contextualize the current tension, human trafficking as a crime or rights violation.

In 2000 the United Nations adopted the *Protocol to Prevent, Suppress and Punish Trafficking in Persons, Especially Women and Children*, supplementing the United Nations Convention against Transnational Organized Crime (2000). The development of the protocol was through a human rights caucus. This reflected a shift in humanitarian priorities—human trafficking was seen as a twenty-first century human rights concern in the international arena. However, in spite of the creation of the protocol through a human rights caucus, the link between human trafficking and human rights was thwarted with tension: The delegates in the human rights caucus could not agree on whether human trafficking was a crime, therefore necessitating a law enforcement instrument, or an issue that should be prioritized under human rights treaties. Eventually the decision was made, and human trafficking is now perceived of as a crime issue.

The human rights component of human trafficking is relegated to being the responsibility of nation-states. Countries like the United States are tasked with ensuring the rights of victims of human trafficking through state policies as well as reinforcing actions to prosecute it as a crime. Therefore, the United States passed the Trafficking Victims Protection Act (2000). The TVPA includes immigration relief for victims of international trafficking and resources to aid victims in stabilization after a life of human trafficking.

Proponents of human trafficking as a human rights concern see victims of human trafficking as victims of rights violation including (extreme) violence, poverty, abuse during migration, or fleeing situations of vulnerability, such as war or political unrest.[1] This approach considers the crime from the perspective of the trafficked person.[2] A human rights approach is an approach that tackles human trafficking from a rights-based approach. The solution is to restore the rights of victims or advocate for their rights as the central response.

However, a human rights approach is not without paradox. Current critiques of human rights approaches contend that it reinforces colonial relations where victims are "othered"—turned into objects as victims who are only known through a narrative of victimhood.[3] We see this in the media coverage of human trafficking. Victim stories are consumed by audiences where they are reduced to numbers, referred to as an amorphous victim or with images that reduce them into objects behind cages or shackled and bound.[4] Images of human trafficking survivors are today's social media update, quickly forgotten the next day. Another problematic aspect of human rights appeals is that it reinforces rescue. The perception is that anti-traffickers are the only real rescuers in an anti-trafficking story. Trafficked people are a part of our everyday lives.[5] And their oppression in particular industries (labor or sexual economies) cannot be delinked from poverty, racism, nationalism, sexist, and patriarchal beliefs and practices.

It is for this reason I call for a critical human rights approach. This approach seeks solidarity across difference. Instead of viewing the anti-trafficker as hero, anti-trafficking endeavors must centralize the victim-witness, the person testifying to a twenty-first century violation; their multiple experiences should shape policy and practice. It also requires moving away from the popular belief of "rescuing victims." To move beyond a rescue mentality, a critical human rights approach is not led by rescuers, but rather, by a coalition of people whose theories and practices are informed by those who are most marginalized in dominant society—people who are seen as the subjects of human trafficking—the victims and survivors of human trafficking.

A critical human rights approach foregrounds the complex conditions that shape human trafficking experiences: race, gender, criminalization, immigration and national origins (and belonging), global economies, class, abilities, and age. Taking lessons from the movement for women's human rights, a critical human rights approach recognizes the need to bridge the political, social, civil, economic, and cultural aspects of human conditions and human rights (not to privilege any in particular, where civil and political rights are oftentimes centralized, at the cost of cultural, economic, and social rights).[6] In doing so, a critical human rights approach reconciles the differing institutional responses that shape trafficked people's experiences. For example, victims of human trafficking may participate in criminalized acts—prostitution, immigration violations, and other crimes of moral turpitude. Legal examples of the challenges surrounding victim complicity and victimhood are seen in cases like *United States v. Dann* where the victim of human trafficking participated in visa fraud and in *United States v. Kang* where some of the victims knowingly entered into sexual economies. Some victims of human trafficking participate in criminal acts as a means to survive, or due to limited options, or because of the failure of a society to address socioeconomic disenfranchisements.

Therefore a critical human rights approach accounts for the conditions and the power dynamics that shape victimhood and criminality. It also does not foreground singular solutions, but rather, complex, multifaceted, and dynamic approaches to this twenty-first century preoccupation and societal ill.

31 - What is the 4P paradigm?

The 4P paradigm (or model) consists of Prevention, Protection, Prosecution, and Partnership. The U.S. Department of State promotes this model as both a national and international framework through which anti-trafficking efforts should be approached. It reminds us the response to human trafficking operates along a spectrum. No single P, no single sector (such as the law enforcement sector), no single agency, and certainly no single person can adequately respond to human trafficking alone.

Viewed at a local level, for example, prevention of trafficking might consist of a MANGO raising public awareness through public events or training professional sectors in how to recognize trafficking. Protection may consist of a local VSP providing housing and services for victims. Prosecution is the responsibility of both federal and local law enforcement agencies that investigate cases and prosecute the traffickers. But law enforcement officers may also be involved in prevention activities, for example, by speaking at public events. And VSPs often play a role in the prosecution of cases by providing the victim with the services and assistance they need for stability so they can be available to assist prosecutors at trial. These routine examples of how agencies from one "P" interact with agencies from another "P" illustrate how most organizations involved in anti-trafficking efforts cannot do their work alone.

This interdependence highlights the importance of the fourth P: Partnership. The most effective responses to trafficking involve working closely with other organizations and individuals. In the example cited above, if the MANGO is training hospital emergency department staff to identify trafficking victims, part of that training must include instructions for reporting a trafficking victim. If the MANGO has partnered with the local police, the police will be aware of this training (perhaps even participating in the training) and will not be caught off guard if they receive a call from the hospital. If the local VSP is housing a victim during the trial phase of prosecution, the attorney and VSP case manager will usually be in regular contact. So the partnerships between agencies—and the individuals involved—are critical to success.

In a broader context, those creating policy or legislation at all levels (local, national, even international) will be most effective if they have strong partnerships among those agencies whose work will be impacted by the policies or legislation enacted.

The essential point is no single sector, agency, or individual can effectively respond to trafficking alone. We need each other. Creating, sustaining, and effectively working within a sphere of partnerships is the most critical aspect of anti-trafficking work. Effectively fighting human trafficking demands a truly integrated effort.

32 - What is a multisector response?

A *multisector* (or *multidisciplinary*) *response* refers to the multiple professional sectors required for a proper and effective response to human trafficking. This term is an important addition to the abolitionist's vocabulary since it is commonly used among agencies involved in anti-trafficking work.

If the 4P paradigm illustrates the potential links between the four areas of anti-trafficking effort, a multisector response with effective partnerships fosters the involvement of many people or organizations with specialized areas of expertise, skills, or specific types of capacities, such as housing for victims. It takes a village, so to speak, to provide the best response possible in a trafficking case.

One simple example helps to illustrate how many different professional disciplines might be involved in providing the services needed by a single victim. Suppose a victim was forced to work as a domestic servant for three years in the United States and is a foreign national whose visa has expired. The case is investigated and prosecuted by federal agencies. Here are the most basic services the victim will need and the professionals and organizations needed to provide them.

- Short-term housing (shelter provider)
- Food and clothing (shelter provider)
- Translation services, if the victim speaks limited English (translator)
- Immigration assistance to address expired visa (immigration attorney)
- Medical assistance (medical doctors)
- Emotional and psychological assistance (doctors, therapists)
- Assistance to collect wages due from the trafficker (civil attorney)

- Assistance to contact family members outside the U.S. (U.S. State Department or NGO)
- Law enforcement to investigate the case (FBI and/or Homeland Security Investigations – HSI)
- Prosecutors (United States Attorney's Office)
- Federal assistance to determine lost wages (U.S. Department of Labor)
- Access to appropriate cultural, ethnic, religious support (VSP, CBO, or FBO)
- Long-term housing while the prosecution proceeds (VSP)
- Case manager who coordinates all of the above on the victim's behalf (VSP)

These are the minimal needs for one person! In cases with additional victims, or victims with complex needs, this list can quickly lengthen. The specialized skills required when responding to human trafficking can be extremely diverse, though not every case requires each specialization. So how do we best coordinate access to all of the standard and potential services needed when responding to an incident of human trafficking? By creating and sustaining anti-trafficking task forces.

33 - What is a human trafficking task force?

In the United States, the term Human Trafficking Task Force was first used by the U.S. Department of Justice in 2004 when they launched a grant program to fund multisector (or multi-disciplinary) teams responding to human trafficking. Today, this program remains a keystone in the federal government's response to trafficking within the United States.

In this particular program, two agencies within the Department of Justice award grants to local agencies; the Office for Victims of Crime awards grants to local VSPs, while the Bureau of Justice Assistance awards grants to local law enforcement agencies. This program is designed with the intention that these two awardees work together closely along with regional representatives from the United States Attorney's Office (USAO), Federal Bureau of Investigation (FBI), and Homeland Security Investigations (HSI). Under this program, over 40 task forces have been funded nationwide, but the number of task forces operating at any one time fluctuates due to a variety of factors, including the challenge of creating and sustaining effective partnerships among the different agencies and individuals involved.

Over time, the term *task force* has become a more generic term for any anti-trafficking, multisector team, regardless of the source of funding. Today, these multisector teams use a variety of terms in the names of their organizations; the most common include *task force, coalition*, or *collaborative*. Regardless of what a multisector team calls itself, the multisector response is considered a best practice worldwide.

A typical task force might include both local and federal investigators and prosecutors (because their authorities differ but are equally necessary) along with a VSP to provide and coordinate victim services. In reality, few VSPs can provide all the services a victim may need, so VSPs, NGOs, FBOs, and CBOs work together to offer a full range of services. These same organizations, or a MANGO partner, can be involved in raising awareness of human trafficking within the community or engaged in training efforts for professionals on the front lines.

As more organizations engage in task forces or other collaborative efforts, institutional and individual differences can make forming and sustaining effective partnerships challenging. In addition, with so many different organizations involved, turnover within these organizations can have a ripple effect which makes sustaining these partnerships challenging. As a result, this type of collaborative work requires those doing the work to possess traits beyond expertise in their professions. It takes patience, adaptability, and other leadership skills to form and sustain effective partnerships.

34 - Why is collaboration so difficult to achieve?

If a multisector response is necessary and no single agency can respond to slavery alone, we must have partnerships to succeed. So why is this collaboration so difficult? Ask anyone involved in the response to trafficking, and the odds are they will say working across agencies and professional sectors can be the most challenging work they encounter.

Collaboration is among the most popular words used today. Politicians state their desire to "collaborate with colleagues across the aisle"; public agency leaders plan to "work in collaboration with local community partners." Everyone wants to do it, but what does it mean to collaborate?

Collaboration should be viewed as something far greater than cooperation or coordination, and we can distinguish the differences by examining how much effort or commitment the work entails and what the final results will accomplish.

Cooperation can require very little commitment, as little as saying, "My organization opposes trafficking, as does yours. We are cooperating in our opposition." Coordination implies we are supporting and complementing one another's efforts and at some level, usually means adjusting what, how, or when we do something to help both of us achieve our goals. In anti-trafficking work, this might include law enforcement sharing information (which they are loath to do with anyone) with a VSP about an upcoming anti-trafficking operation so the VSP can be prepared to assist victims.

Collaboration goes beyond cooperation or coordination. Collaboration seeks to create long-term relationships and new solutions for complex problems. Looking at how task forces are organized and the diversity of professionals and organizations needed to respond to trafficking, it is clear challenges are inevitable. In the earliest stages of task force creation, establishing a process for group decision-making is critical.

Various factors can contribute to this difficulty. First, each agency's institutional decision-making system differs. For instance, law enforcement has a clear hierarchal structure and applauds quick decision-making skills, standards that may not transfer well to non-law enforcement organizations. Some organizations may have outdated systems that need to be adapted in order to offer an improved response. For example, a VSP who in the past has worked alone might need to adapt to work with other organizations so together they can more effectively serve the special needs of trafficking victims. Other barriers can include competition over funding, "turf wars" over which organization will handle specific duties, and last but not least, agreeing upon the agency that will be seen as the leader of the task force.

On top of these institutional factors, the individuals responsible for performing the work can bring their own impediments to collaboration, including a lack of desire to engage with organizations and individuals outside their own sector, a lack of belief that trafficking exists within the community they serve, or an inability to envision new ways of addressing problems. Individuals who lack patience or who cannot view problems from another's perspective will find collaborative work especially challenging. Often these problems fester because in order to address them, some level of collaboration must exist in the first place!

So what is the best way to stack the odds in favor of success? First, those selected for collaborative work should be chosen for their collaborative skills, not necessarily their technical skills. A task force investigator who is not interested in collaboration should focus on investigating cases; another person from the police agency can engage in the collaborative work. The same can be said for VSPs, NGOs, or CBOs involved in the task force. Many good case managers and public outreach coordinators perform their jobs exceptionally well but don't want to take on collaborative roles and should not be forced into a role they don't desire. Also, working with others in a collaborative environment takes time—a lot of time. This requirement must be recognized by both the person engaged in collaborative work and by their supervisors and managers.

Organizations involved in anti-trafficking work realize that to be effective, they may have to change their policies and procedures to adapt to the greater good of the task force. Good collaborators can think creatively and see past the effort required to create change—to the increased effectiveness and efficiency that will result. Most importantly, good collaborators are willing to work with others and learn from them, in an effort to find new solutions to complex problems.

The level of inter-agency and cross-sector collaboration necessary for an effective response to human trafficking is uniquely demanding. Everyone involved must understand the challenges of this collaboration. My colleague Kirsten Foot examines this topic in detail in her book, *Collaborating Against Human Trafficking: Cross-Sector Challenges and Practices*.[7] Kirsten's book is highly recommended for further study.

35 - What is the Human Trafficking Task Force e-Guide?

This e-guide could be listed only in the Resources section at the end of the book, but it deserves mention here. No comparable resource exists, and although it primarily addresses investigators, prosecutors, and VSPs, it should be examined by everyone involved in the response to trafficking.

The Human Trafficking Task Force e-Guide is an online resource for the creation and operation of anti-trafficking task forces. The e-guide is produced through the efforts of the U.S. Department of Justice's Office for Justice Programs, the Bureau of Justice Assistance, and the Office for Victims of Crime. While based upon the experience of federally-funded task forces, the e-guide is designed to be a resource for all collaborative task forces, regardless of funding or federal agency participation.

The e-guide addresses task force creation, leadership, and collaborative structure and includes detailed information on investigating and prosecuting cases and providing comprehensive victim services. In this regard, the e-guide is an excellent resource for individual investigators, prosecutors, and those working directly with victims to meet their needs. The e-guide also provides tools and exemplars useful for collaborative work along with updates on trafficking incidents, legislation, and other helpful news.

- https://www.ovcttac.gov/taskforceguide/eguide/

36 - What is the National Human Trafficking Resource Center?

Guest Contributor: Sarah Jakiel
Sarah Jakiel is the Chief Programs Officer of Polaris and has been working in the nonprofit sector for a decade.

Guest Contributor: Nicole Moler
Nicole Moler is the Director of the National Human Trafficking Resource Center (NHTRC), the national, 24/7, confidential, anti-trafficking hotline and resource center serving victims and survivors of human trafficking and the anti-trafficking community in the United States.

The TVPA authorizes the department of Health and Human Services (HHS) to conduct public awareness on the issue of human trafficking. Since FY 2004, as a part of their Rescue and Restore Campaign, HHS has funded the operation of a 24-hour, toll-free, national hotline and resource center serving victims and survivors of human trafficking and the anti-trafficking community in the United States. Originally titled the Trafficking Information and Referral Hotline and later renamed the National Human Trafficking Resource Center (NHTRC) in FY 2007, HHS originally contracted with Lockheed Martin to operate the hotline between FY 2004-2007. During this time, Covenant House, New York staffed the hotline through a sub-contract with Lockheed Martin.

In FY 2008, Polaris was granted responsibility for operating the NHTRC through a cooperative agreement with the Anti-Trafficking in Persons Division (ATIP) in the Office of Refugee Resettlement within HHS. Polaris is a non-profit, non-governmental anti-trafficking organization and a leader in the global fight to eradicate modern slavery and restore freedom to survivors of human trafficking. Polaris began operating the hotline on December 7, 2007. Under Polaris's leadership, the mission of the NHTRC is to provide human trafficking victims and survivors with access to critical support and services to get help and stay safe, and to equip the anti-trafficking community with the tools to effectively combat all forms of human trafficking.

The NHTRC serves four key functions at the national level by providing a confidential crisis and tip line, a comprehensive resource and technical assistance center, a trafficking-specific referral and response network, and a repository of hotline data that allows for the identification of human trafficking trends across the country. The NHTRC serves victims and survivors of all demographics and all forms of human trafficking as well as friends and family, law enforcement, service providers, government actors, community coalitions, practitioners and advocates in human trafficking and related fields as well as the general public and those wishing to learn more. Each call is focused on the individual and their unique needs. Callers are encouraged to understand their rights and the options available to them. The NHTRC supports the caller's right to choose what next steps to take, including whether or not to access services or report information about his/her experience to law enforcement. Call Specialists work with the caller to explore all available options; the NHTRC will not take action without the consent of the caller, except in circumstances of suspected child abuse or imminent danger to the caller or others.

The NHTRC serves as a central access point where callers can connect to diverse forms of human trafficking-specific assistance and resources 24 hours per day, confidentially, anywhere in the U.S., and in their native language. These services include emergency crisis response and assistance; localized referrals for social and legal services; tip reporting; general support for survivors and their friends and family; training, technical assistance, and capacity building tools; national and statewide hotline statistics on human trafficking cases; a resource library of anti-trafficking materials and training tools; and opportunities for community engagement, peer-to-peer connections, and volunteer service. The NHTRC offers three different access points to help meet the diverse needs of the vulnerable populations they serve, including a toll-free, multi-lingual hotline answered live 24 hours a day, 7 days a week, 365 days a year; an email account; and an online tip reporting mechanism. Through research and constituent engagement, Polaris learned that SMS texting capacity was likely to have significant and unique potential for safely reaching victims in need. Polaris launched the BeFree Textline in March 2013 to complement the efforts of the NHTRC.

The NHTRC and BeFree Textline serve constituents through strong partnerships with key stakeholders at the local and national level. The NHTRC has built a robust network of more than 3,200 service providers, government stakeholders, law enforcement officials, task forces, coalitions, and other key partners equipped to meet the diverse needs of victims and survivors of human trafficking, including shelter, transportation, legal assistance, counseling, case management, and much more.

The national hotline is only effective when strong partnerships are in place at the local level. The NHTRC has built more than 250 individualized response protocols with trusted local, state, and federal law enforcement, government agencies, and service providers in communities across the country. These protocols are designed in collaboration with local actors and support the existing local anti-trafficking infrastructure. The NHTRC does not take the place of local actors or the local on-the-ground response and does not provide direct victim services or investigate tips. Instead, the NHTRC provides a national scope, 24-hour infrastructure, comprehensive referral network, and technical expertise on all forms of human trafficking which allows the NHTRC to connect individuals in need, any time of day, anywhere in the country with the agency best equipped to help. NHTRC staff members regularly solicit input from peers and partners in the field as well as survivors to continually improve the quality and effectiveness of our services and meet the evolving needs of our constituents.

Does it work?

The NHTRC's experience has proven that a national anti-trafficking hotline is a critical component of an effective national response to human trafficking, specifically by increasing access to critical services for victims and survivors of human trafficking, providing law enforcement with information about potential cases of human trafficking, and collecting data to inform local and national prevention and intervention efforts. The hotline's impact can be measured in a variety of ways. Between December 2007, when Polaris assumed operation of the hotline, and October 2015, the NHTRC fielded nearly 180,000 signals (calls, emails, tip reports, text conversations). Since then, volume has increased steadily every year, with notable spikes in communities actively publicizing the NHTRC hotline through outreach and awareness campaigns as well as through mandatory posting laws. In 2008, the NHTRC received just under 6,000 calls—an average of 500 calls per month. In 2014, the NHTRC received nearly 34,000 calls or approximately 2,800 calls per month. Of particular note, calls directly from victims and survivors have increased considerably over the years, comprising 5% of callers (where this information is known) in 2008 and reaching 16% in 2015. For the BeFree Textline, this number has reached as high as 33% of those reaching out for help. During this same time period, the NHTRC has responded to more than 23,000 reports of potential sex and labor trafficking cases involving all populations of victims and has reported more than 6,500 cases to law enforcement partners for investigation and immediate assistance to victims in crisis situations. The NHTRC has also directly supported over 350 communities in building an effective response to human trafficking.

The NHTRC has reached a level of saturation within the U.S. response that has allowed it to continue to increase volume without substantive financial investment in marketing. Creating a single, memorable number that can be shared by any and every stakeholder in the anti-trafficking field has pushed the hotline to be viewed as a "community good." It is publicized by all federal agencies, with particular success through the "Know Your Rights" pamphlet created and distributed by the Department of State; it is included in local and community-based campaigns; it is networked with other national hotlines that serve survivors of domestic violence, runaway and homeless youth, and other similar groups in order to cross refer vulnerable callers; it is used by healthcare providers, child protection workers, and state-level enforcement agencies; it is promoted through national and state-level legislation; and it can be used by any individual trying to raise the profile of this issue. Getting the number out and making it as accessible as possible is the first step in reaching victims where they are.

In an environment of hidden crime, inadequate statistics, and low levels of self-reporting, the NHTRC has begun to carve out a picture of human trafficking in the United States that is driven by hard data. It has created access to assistance for more victims of human trafficking than any other single entity in the world. By capturing information about how and where human trafficking occurs, the NHTRC has been able to begin to understand the various types of sex and labor trafficking happening in the U.S. and is better able to decipher common threads of vulnerability among victims, gaps in services in communities that lack an effective and institutionalized response, and those structures and institutions that traffickers exploit in order to commit the crime.

The NHTRC hotline has built a trusted, victim-centered, national safety net that provides victims the help they need to get and stay safe so that more survivors of human trafficking can get out of slavery and vulnerable populations are equipped with information and resources to reduce their risk to human trafficking. This model is being replicated in countries around the world in order to increase victim identification and access to services, collect and share promising practices for building effective prevention and intervention efforts, and drive substantive tips and intelligence to trained law enforcement that can lead to prosecutions.

Should local agencies have their own hotline?

Trafficking is a complex crime and requires a well-coordinated, knowledgeable, and victim-centered response. Since assuming operations of the hotline in 2007, stakeholders in diverse communities across the country have reached out to Polaris for guidance as they are exploring the possibility of building local or statewide hotlines. Polaris has recommended use of the NHTRC hotline in order to allow communities to concentrate their efforts and resources where they are most needed and will have the greatest impact—building a coordinated and comprehensive local response to cases of human trafficking. The NHTRC strives to provide every community with 24-hour response capacity which in turn allows them to invest limited resources in rapid response structures that will take the next critical step of providing direct support to victims on the ground. The NHTRC works in partnership with local communities—each providing a critical component of an effective response.

Ultimately, most communities across the U.S. have opted to utilize the NHTRC as their state hotline, and some have transitioned over to the NHTRC after testing out the possibility of operating a local hotline. It can be valuable for local agencies to operate hotlines serving as intake lines for existing and potential clients to access services and/or to activate local crisis response protocols. The NHTRC plays a role in supporting smaller local organizations that don't have capacity to operate 24/7. Many local organizations and local hotlines have routed calls to the NHTRC after hours and on weekends or when funding wanes. In this way, the NHTRC acts as a permanent back-up support system. For those that operate local or statewide hotlines, the NHTRC has developed referral and reporting protocols to ensure that we are working in tandem to best address the needs of all victims. The national hotline does not replace local services; it simply acts as a centralized venue to triage calls and direct them to the appropriate on-the-ground providers. The NHTRC serves as a resource not just for victims of trafficking but also for service providers and law enforcement seeking technical assistance, resources, referrals outside of their jurisdiction/service area, and general support.

Trafficking cases can span multiple locations, and trafficking survivors often seek assistance outside of the city where they have been trafficked. Human trafficking victims are also frequently moved, and they may not be able to call a local hotline if they are out of the service area, which can provide delays in accessing assistance. The national scope of the NHTRC allows it to manage complex, long-term, and multi-jurisdictional cases and provide consistent responses and communication to callers even when they change locations, when the case requires a nuanced or unusual referral procedure, or when a case spans weeks or months and includes multiple victims.

The NHTRC has the infrastructure and resources to effectively assist victims, survivors, and those working in the anti-trafficking field 24 hours a day, 7 days a week, anywhere in the U.S. and U.S. territories, in more than 200 languages. The NHTRC serves as a central access point for all inquiries related to human trafficking and has the capacity to triage the call and assess the caller's needs in order to determine the most appropriate resource(s) to fulfill the caller's request. The NHTRC has the staff capacity to respond to multiple calls simultaneously which means it can devote one or more staff exclusively to managing a crisis call while responding to other incoming calls. The NHTRC collects key data from each hotline call so that it can track trends and share in-depth non-personally identifying information with local actors, thus avoiding regional information silos and enhancing local and national prevention and intervention efforts. Centralized data collection allows us to detect new trends and identify promising practices and gaps in trafficking networks, in law enforcement response, and in victim services. Standardized data collection ensures that all calls/cases are viewed from the same lens. The NHTRC also tracks and reports back on the impact of individual local and national awareness campaigns, based on calls generated through these initiatives.

Responding to human trafficking effectively is incredibly challenging and resource intensive and parsing out each phase of response has immense value when investment from state and federal government remains drastically distant from meeting the needs on the ground. Continuing to support a national hotline effort provides a critical backstop for providers across the country and continues to allow for a national view on the issue of human trafficking as it evolves across states and time.

37 - What are the J/TIP Office and the TIP Report?

Guest Contributor: Alejandra Acevedo
Alejandra Acevedo has over 7 years of experience related to combatting human trafficking. She has worked on this issue in various roles with non-governmental organizations, the government, and the private sector and is currently a Human Trafficking Training and Technical Assistance Specialist for the Office for Victims of Crime Training and Technical Assistance Center (OVC TTAC).

The Trafficking Victims Protection Act (TVPA) of 2000 authorized the establishment of the Department of State's Office to Monitor and Combat Trafficking in Persons (commonly referred to as the J/TIP office, or simply, J/TIP). The Office leads the United States' domestic and international engagement against human trafficking and is organized into four sections: Reports and Political Affairs, International Programs, Public Engagement, and Resource Management and Planning.[8]

Reports and Political Affairs

The Reports and Political Affairs (RPA) section's primary role is to "engage foreign governments on human trafficking issues" while promoting the 4P approach: prevention, protection, prosecution, and partnership.[9] The RPA section also assesses the anti-trafficking efforts of countries and territories, including the United States, in the annual Trafficking in Persons (TIP) Report. The TIP Report is the "U.S. government's principal diplomatic tool and the world's most comprehensive resource on governmental anti-trafficking efforts." Each country analysis is based on a government's efforts to comply with the "minimum standards for the elimination of trafficking" found in Section 108 of the TVPA and includes recommendations consistent with anti-trafficking standards set out in the *United Nations Protocol to Prevent, Suppress, and Punish Trafficking in Persons, especially Women and Children*.[10] The RPA section uses information reported to the Office from U.S. diplomatic posts and domestic agencies as well as research gathered through meetings with government officials, local and international non-governmental organization (NGO) representatives, officials, international organizations, journalists, academics,[11] and survivors, to rank each country's government on its anti-trafficking efforts using the following tier ranking system:

The Tiers[12]

Tier 1
Countries whose governments fully comply with the TVPA's minimum standards.

Tier 2
Countries whose governments do not fully comply with the TVPA's minimum standards but are making significant efforts to bring themselves into compliance with those standards.

Tier 2 Watch List
Countries whose governments do not fully comply with the TVPA's minimum standards but are making significant efforts to bring themselves into compliance with those standards AND:

a. The **absolute number of victims** of severe forms of trafficking is very significant or is significantly increasing;

b. There is a **failure to provide evidence of increasing efforts** to combat severe forms of trafficking in persons from the previous year; or

c. The determination that a country is making significant efforts to bring itself into compliance with minimum standards was based on **commitments by the country to take additional future steps over the next year.**

Tier 3
Countries whose governments do not fully comply with the minimum standards and are not making significant efforts to do so.

International Programs

The International Programs (IP) section's primary role is to administer foreign assistance funds to combat human trafficking. Administered funds are awarded in the form of grants to international and non-governmental organizations whose projects address the 4Ps. The IP section also performs onsite monitoring of projects and provides targeted training and technical assistance to support grantees in meeting project goals.[13]

Public Engagement

The Office's Public Engagement (PE) section's primary role is to work "with Congress, the media, NGOs, other U.S. government agencies, multilateral organizations, corporations, academia, research institutes, and civil society to raise awareness about human trafficking and the U.S. government's anti-trafficking efforts and to build partnerships to help strengthen those efforts."[14] The PE section also supports the Secretary of State in their role as Chair of the President's Interagency Task Force to Monitor and Combat Trafficking in Persons (PITF). The PITF is a cabinet-level entity, created by the TVPA, which consists of 14 departments and agencies across the federal government that coordinates U.S. government-wide efforts to combat human trafficking.[15] The PE section includes the Multilateral Affairs team whose purpose is to engage and represent the Office on matters related to the United Nations, the International Labour Organization, the European Union, the Organization for Security and Cooperation in Europe, the Organization of American States, and the Regional Conference on Migration.[16]

Resource Management and Planning

The Resource Management and Planning (RMP) section's primary goal is "to provide management support to the Office, including strategic planning, performance management, evaluation oversight, budget formulation and execution for foreign assistance and state operations resources, human resource liaison services, general services, travel, and contract support."[17]

CHAPTER 4

Responding to Human Trafficking: Victims and Their Needs

The moment the slave resolves that he will no longer be a slave, his fetters fall. Freedom and slavery are mental states.
GANDHI

As we have seen, the needs of a trafficking victim can be extensive and may require a diverse team of experts and providers. The need for support services may last months or even years. While addressing all of the potential needs of a victim is beyond the scope of this book, every abolitionist—regardless of role — should be familiar with the basic guidelines for providing these services.

38 - What is a victim-centered response?

The term "victim-centered response" first appeared in the Trafficking Victims Protection Act and is a fundamental standard of response. A victim-centered response should be understood and adopted by every person involved in anti-trafficking work, regardless of role.

The Human Trafficking Task Force e-Guide states, "In a victim-centered approach, the victim's wishes, safety, and well-being take priority in all matters and procedures."[1] In other words, every person and agency involved places the victim's wishes before their own, and policies and procedures used in the response to trafficking remain flexible to ensure the best possible treatment of the victim.

For example, the TVPA states that central to the victim-centered response, victims who choose not to cooperate with law enforcement for the prosecution of their case cannot be denied the rights and reliefs spelled out in the TVPA. Specifically, the TVPA grants immigration relief to trafficking victims, and a pre-TVPA concern was that law enforcement officers might withhold the immigration relief from victims so as to coerce them into assisting with the prosecution. However, not every victim of a crime desires to have their case prosecuted. In the same respect, not every victim of a crime wants to receive all of the reliefs to which they may be entitled. In the complex environment of offering services to victims of trafficking, it can be tempting to push something on to a victim they simply don't want, for example, offering local housing to a victim when what they desire is to return home—wherever that may be. We must, in these cases, ask ourselves, "Does this action benefit my goals or the victim's?"

Being mindful of a victim-centered response also requires a framework for developing policies and procedures, whether they are law enforcement procedures, service provider procedures, or other policies. Establishing victim-centered protocols can become a challenge when multiple agencies are involved in the response, especially when adopting policies which may have been created before the advent of victim-centered principles.

To be victim-centered is to be aware that our professional actions and agency policies and procedures can impact the victims we are trying to serve. Everyone involved in the process should be an advocate for the victim, avoiding re-traumatizing the victim and engaging with the victim throughout—and beyond—their experience of enslavement. The victim is the most important person in the trafficking-response equation.

39 - What is a trauma-informed response?

This term, often encountered in the anti-trafficking community, is not specific to victims of trafficking. A trauma-informed responder recognizes the impact trauma has on victims of all crimes and the impediment trauma poses on the victim's path to recovery. At its core, a trauma-informed response actively seeks to use processes, procedures, and policies to help prevent re-traumatizing the victim.

Being trauma-informed also implies understanding how trauma impacts those who are assisting victims. Professionals, including law enforcement, service providers, and others who have regular contact with victims of crime, cannot help but suffer some degree of trauma over the course of their careers.

The trauma of victimization does not go away the moment the traumatic incident ends. Victims of violence are impacted to some degree for the rest of their lives.

40 - What are the unique needs of a trafficking victim?

Guest Contributor: Kiricka Yarbough Smith

Kiricka Yarbough Smith is a consultant who works on a variety of anti-trafficking efforts, including working as an investigator on the University of North Carolina, School of Social Work's project addressing child trafficking in the welfare system. Kiricka also serves as faculty for the Futures Without Violence project on building collaboration to address human trafficking in domestic violence and sexual assault cases, funded by the U.S. Department of Justice's Office on Violence Against Women.

Human trafficking is first and foremost a violation of an individual's human right to freedom. For many trafficking victims, recovery and rehabilitation from the cumulative trauma of trafficking depends on the restoration of their physical and mental health and sense of humanity. Using a victim-centered approach is essential to this process of restoration.

When serving these victims, professional staff and volunteers must be cognizant of the physical and emotional abuse victims have suffered. The exploitation suffered by victims is extensive, pervading body and mind; recovery is a long and arduous process that can be facilitated or hindered by the types of interactions victims have with law enforcement and service providers. A victim-centered approach uses patience, empathy, and compassion for victims while responding to their needs.

8 Key Components of the Victim-Centered Approach

1. **Understanding the Complexity of Trafficking Cases:** The victim-centered approach requires that all actors involved in a trafficking case understand the complexity of trafficking, how traffickers entrap their victims, and how mislabeling victims as offenders undermines efforts to eliminate trafficking and rescue victims.[2] Es-

cape from trafficking does not guarantee a direct road to recovery; it is a long-term, complex process.

2. **Confidentiality:** Service providers should ensure that survivors are informed and aware of the confidentiality requirements that apply to all persons employed by the support agency. This information is critical so that survivors are assured of their right to confidentiality and can make an informed decision regarding disclosure. Forms for Informed Consent and Consent to Release Information must be provided to the survivor in their primary language.

3. **Working with Interpreters:** To facilitate communication between referral/support agencies and survivors and to ensure survivors are able to fully understand their rights and entitlements, it is crucial that interpreters are available in all cases where English is not the survivor's first language.

4. **Health Needs:** Survivors of human trafficking often develop a host of health conditions, including physical injuries, sexual health problems, chronic somatic health issues, and long-term mental health difficulties. Chronic health conditions can include fatigue, weight loss, headaches, dizzy spells, loss of memory, fainting, stomach and abdominal pain, chest and heart pain, breathing difficulty, back pain, and vision and ear problems. Emotional difficulties can range from severe anxiety to depression, panic attacks, suicidal ideation, and various forms of post-traumatic stress disorders.

   - *Substance use.* Many victims will be dependent on drugs and alcohol, as they had often been coerced and forced to use these substances by their traffickers. Victims may need treatment to help end their dependency on drugs and alcohol.

   - *Access to sexual health services.* Being aware of and sensitive to the extreme trauma inflicted by a single act of rape is essential to recognizing the enduring impact of repeated rape on trafficking survivors, whether male or female. Many survivors will have difficulty disclosing rape and sexual abuse due to shame and fear of stigma or shunning from their communities and families. All survivors should be provided with access to counseling as a routine part of sexual health screening and given immediate access to their local rape crisis center or child advocacy center. Survivors should be encouraged to consider making a report to police in parallel with sexual health screening. In all cases, any action or reports to the police should be taken only with the survivor's informed consent.

- *Pregnant survivors of trafficking.* Women may become pregnant or give birth to children while under the control of traffickers or after having escaped from traffickers. These survivors need special care and assistance whether their pregnancy is a result of rape or consensual sex with a person not involved with their trafficking situation. Mothers, especially those who have children from rape and/or do not have a partner, may need psychological support and contact with professionals who understand the complexity of trafficking-related trauma. If the survivor chooses to raise her child, this psychological support is especially important to help a traumatized survivor cope with the added stressors associated with caring for a child.

  Addressing the health care needs of trafficking survivors using an integrated, long-term care approach is essential for trafficked women who are or become pregnant and/or have children. Service providers working with female trafficking survivors should ensure these women have access to appropriate counseling and support to enable them to make independent and informed choices about all aspects of reproduction, including contraception, conception (including fertility issues), pregnancy, abortion, childbirth, and adoption.

- *Developmental disabilities.* All age groups require a comprehensive clinical assessment for mental health and cognitive needs. The comprehensive clinical assessment will dictate referrals for therapy for behavioral, psychological, medical, physical, and occupational needs.

- *Comprehensive clinical assessment.* Survivors in crisis should be assessed regarding their current mental and behavioral health needs, including whether they present a risk to themselves or others. A comprehensive clinical assessment includes an assessment of suicide risk, homicide risk, psychosis, substance use/addiction, psychiatric medication use, and a psychological evaluation.

5. **Addressing Safety:** An initial safety assessment and safety plan should be completed during the screening and intake process. After screening and intake are completed and ongoing service providers have engaged with survivors, the safety plan should be reviewed and revised as needed.

    - *Safety planning for survivors.* Safety plans should be specific to the survivor with respect to known risk factors, legal sanctions, and age; safety plans should be developed in collaboration with the placement provider, child welfare worker, law enforcement, family, and other natural supports in the community. Victims need a safe place to recover from their trauma where they do not feel singled out due to their unique experiences.

6. **Independent Living Services:** Regardless of age, survivors will need to develop life skills to help them successfully transition and integrate into their commu-

nities and live independently. A life skills assessment should be conducted to determine the survivor's interests, strengths, and abilities. The following life skill domains should be assessed and included in planning:

- Education or vocational trainin
- Housing access and maintenance skill
- Financial literacy skills
- Employment and job-related skills
- Accessing transportation systems
- Positive coping skills

7. **The Survivor Support Plan:** The survivor support plan should be based on the outcomes of the individual survivor's risk and needs assessments and prepared with the direct involvement of the survivor. During this process, it is crucial to establish trust and mutually agreed-upon objectives, and to avoid making any promises or guarantees to survivors that might not be possible to fulfill.

8. **Ongoing Housing and Placement Considerations:** If housing is to be provided to survivors of trafficking, make sure the housing is safe, secure, fit for the intended purpose and occupants, and in a confidential location. The victim should also receive an explanation on the importance of keeping their address and phone number confidential from past acquaintances that might be associated with the trafficker.

Special Considerations

Male Victims: According to the Polaris Project, males make up 5% of sex trafficking victims and 40% of labor trafficking victims. While females make up the larger majority, there are still those smaller percentages of men who are also affected and require the same attention given to females. Since men are taught to hide their feelings, male trafficking victims find it difficult to ask for and receive help. Male human trafficking is often unacknowledged, so it comes as no surprise that there is a lack of services for male victims. Some of the most important services needed by male victims include housing and counseling.

LGBTQ Community: Youth who identify as lesbian, gay, bisexual, transgender, queer, or questioning (LGBTQ) may be disproportionately affected by human trafficking. They face higher rates of discrimination and homelessness, making them especially vulnerable to traffickers. When LGBTQ trafficking victims seek services or go through the criminal justice system, they are often penalized for their sexual orientation or gender identity. Even when community members and service providers do want to help, they frequently lack the training needed to recognize trafficking or how to effectively and compassionately assist LGBTQ youth. If the basic needs of LGBTQ youth continue to go unmet, these young people face a greater risk of returning to their trafficking situations.

41 - What legal processes may impact a trafficking survivor?

Guest Contributor: Cindy Liou

Cindy C. Liou, Esq. is a consultant, trainer, author, and attorney who practices law in the areas of human trafficking, immigration law, family law, and domestic violence. Recently, she was the Director of the Human Trafficking Project at Asian Pacific Islander Legal Outreach and the Co-Chair of the Policy Committee of the Freedom Network to Empower Trafficked and Enslaved Persons (USA).

Due to the breadth and complexity of the ways that human trafficking can occur, a single human trafficking survivor may encounter multiple legal processes. How the legal system works in each area of law depends on the jurisdiction of the case (international, federal, state, county, city, tribal, or military) and the type of legal issue at hand. A trafficking survivor may require assistance with a wide range of legal processes, from navigating the criminal justice system to understanding immigration law, family law, civil litigation and other legal procedures. The following is a general overview of the main legal processes that a trafficking survivor may require assistance with.

Criminal Justice System

In criminal cases, the government is usually investigating or prosecuting someone on behalf of the community to penalize them for violating laws. Trafficking survivors tend to encounter the criminal justice system as a victim-witness or as a criminal defendant/juvenile offender in a case.

Victims are often called upon as witnesses in these cases and frequently serve as the only form of "evidence" in the case against the traffickers. Victims should be able to exercise victims' rights under U.S. federal law and certain state laws. Basic victims' rights, which are personal rights of the victim, include the:

- Right to be treated with respect and sensitivity, right to protection (protective orders, relocation),
- Right to apply for compensation with state funds (medical and therapy expenses, lost wages),
- Right to criminal restitution to hold the traffickers directly responsible for financial harm they have caused the victims (lost wages, property loss),
- Right to be informed (arrest of trafficker, dismissal of charges, sentencing, probation, appeals, release of trafficker), and
- Right not to be excluded from and to be able to speak at the criminal justice proceedings (participate in hearings, sentencing, submitting victim impact statements).

Trafficking survivors may also be coerced or forced into committing criminal acts in the course of their trafficking situation. In these cases, they might be arrested, charged, and/or convicted of committing crimes. Some examples include criminal charges of prostitution, possession or sale of drugs, and entering the country without proper documentation. In these cases, trafficking survivors need criminal defense attorneys and possibly immigration removal defense attorneys to counsel them about their rights through the process as well as advocate for their case as trafficking victims. They may also need legal advocates during their probation period. Minors that are caught offending and committing crimes enter juvenile delinquency systems that have specific procedures for working with youth.

Criminal convictions can prevent trafficking survivors from important things integral to their healing process, including obtaining employment, receiving medical care, furthering education, receiving housing, obtaining financial assistance and benefits, and obtaining immigration relief. Some states have now passed post-conviction relief laws, including trafficking-specific expungement and vacatur laws to help survivors "clean" their criminal record.

Immigration Law

Many trafficking survivors are foreign nationals who require immigration assistance. Without immigration status, they may face deportation, inability to work and earn income, and lack of access to housing, benefits, medical, and mental health services. They may need assistance in applying for immigration status, deportation defense, obtaining documents, and reunifying with their family members. If they want to return to their country of origin, they may also need assistance with repatriation.

Civil Litigation

Trafficking survivors are also often eligible to seek financial justice for the forced labor or exploitation they have been subjected to. This is typically done through civil litigation and civil actions, which are legal disputes that are not brought in criminal court, and what is sought is usually money damages. Unlike criminal law, the trafficking survivor can be the main plaintiff who "drives" the legal process in bringing a lawsuit against their trafficker in civil court. These lawsuits can be brought by trafficking survivors parallel with criminal prosecutions or on their own even if there is no criminal investigation. There is sometimes a possibility to recover greater money damages in civil litigation cases than in the amount of money that can be recovered through criminal restitution or crime victims' compensation funds. These civil claims may be based on lost wages, workplace injuries, sexual harassment, sexual assault, breach (breaking) of contract, and discrimination in the course of their trafficking. Additionally, sometimes certain civil money damages and criminal restitution orders are taxable, and so trafficking survivors may also need counseling on tax laws.

Family Law

Human trafficking cases often intersect with domestic violence and sexual assault. Trafficking survivors sometimes need assistance in family law matters, especially in cases where the traffickers are family members or the traffickers and survivors have children together. In these cases, trafficking survivors may need legal assistance with obtaining restraining orders or protective orders, divorce, and child custody and visitation.

Benefits

Supporting trafficking survivors requires financial assistance in their day to day living, medical and mental health expenses, and daily expenses. Trafficking survivors may need assistance with accessing local, state, and federal benefits. The benefits available to them may also be dependent on their income, legal status, marital status, age, and other complicated factors. Sometimes civil money damages or criminal restitution can negatively affect trafficking survivors from receiving public benefits. Thus, a trafficking survivor may need to consult a benefits attorney for assistance in structuring their money damages properly.

Other Legal Needs

Because every trafficking case is different, there are many other areas of law that a trafficking survivor may need assistance in—the list is endless and each trafficking survivor must be individually considered. Youth may require additional legal representation in guardianship proceedings, education, and school issues (placement, suspension, tuition). Many trafficking survivors often face housing problems, such as securing placement, handling eviction, or breaking their leases early to leave a trafficking situation. Trafficking survivors with disabilities, for example, may need assistance in enforcing disability discrimination laws. Some survivors may need help maintaining the privacy of their medical records or applying for fee waivers for medical care. Some trafficking survivors may request name changes for safety concerns, and some transgender trafficking survivors may request name and gender changes.

42 - What kinds of immigration relief are available to foreign-national survivors?

Guest Contributor: Lynette M. Parker

Lynette M. Parker is Clinical Faculty (Immigration Practice Area) at the Alexander Community Law Center, Santa Clara University School of Law. She is a member of the South Bay Coalition to End Human Trafficking as well as the Santa Clara County (CA) Human Trafficking Commission.

What is the purpose behind immigration relief for foreign-national survivors?

Immigration relief provides critical support to survivors of human trafficking by giving them stability and certainty in their lives. It makes possible permission to work legally, guarantees access to United States courts for pursuing justice and to services for healing, and protects survivors from having to return to their countries to face the danger of retaliation or re-trafficking. Immigration relief also aids law enforcement by allowing survivors to stay in the U.S. to assist with an investigation and prosecution of the traffickers.

What is Continued Presence (CP) and why is it important?

Continued Presence is a form of relief where Immigration acknowledges the presence of someone in the U.S. but chooses not to remove that person from the U.S. at the request of law enforcement. CP is valid, with work authorization, for one year. It also triggers federal public benefits.

What is T Nonimmigrant Status, what are the required elements for a T visa, and why is it important?

Nonimmigrant visas are temporary permission to come to or stay in the U.S. for a specific purpose for a set amount of time. Nonimmigrant visas include foreign student visas, tourist visas, and temporary work visas. T visas are nonimmigrant visas available to victims of severe forms of human trafficking.

To apply for T visas, survivors must show: 1) that they are victims of a severe form of human trafficking; 2) that they are present in the U.S. or at a port of entry because of the trafficking; 3) that they have complied with reasonable requests of law enforcement for assistance in the investigation or prosecution of the trafficking; and 4) that they will suffer extreme hardship involving unusual or severe harm if removed from the U.S. To be present because of trafficking does not always mean entry to the U.S. for that reason. Persons can be recruited and forced to work in the U.S. without crossing a border. The T visa is a possibility as long as the survivor can establish that he or she remains present in the U.S. for reasons tied to the trafficking—e.g., to assist with law enforcement; to pursue civil or administrative remedies; or to receive medical, mental health, or other services for harm caused by the trafficking. If discovered at a port of entry, the survivor may not have reached his or her ultimate destination, but the trafficker had the intent to bring the person into the U.S. for the purposes of forcing the person to provide labor or services in the U.S.

There are some exceptions to the requirement that the survivor comply with reasonable requests of law enforcement for assistance. Any survivor under 18 years of age is not required to demonstrate compliance. Persons unable to comply due to physical or psychological trauma are also exempt. Extreme hardship factors include age and personal circumstance, likelihood that the trafficker will retaliate against the person if he or she returns to his or her home country, likelihood the survivor will be re-trafficked, and the possibility the survivor will be shunned or ostracized by the community in his or her home country. In the case of likelihood of retaliation or re-trafficking, survivors can show the inability of their governments to protect them.

T visas grant legal status, as well as work authorization, for four years. They can be extended beyond the four years under specific circumstances. Between the third and fourth year of the visa, it is possible to apply for permanent residence (green card).

It is also possible for certain family members of survivors to receive T visas and work authorization. This is true if the family member is inside or outside of the U.S. As with CP, T visas trigger federal public benefits.

What is U Nonimmigrant Status, what are the required elements for a U, and why is it important?

U Nonimmigrant visas are similar to T Nonimmigrant visas. U visas are available for victims of certain listed crimes in the U.S. and are also valid with work authorization for four years.

To apply for U visas, survivors must show: 1) they have been a victim of one of the listed crimes, either in the U.S. or that the crime has violated U.S. law; 2) they possess information concerning the criminal activity; 3) they have been, are being, or are likely to be helpful to law enforcement investigating or prosecuting the criminal activity; **and** 4) they suffered substantial physical or mental abuse as a result of being a victim of the crime. The listed crimes include rape, torture, trafficking, sexual exploitation, involuntary servitude, kidnapping, slave trade, false imprisonment, and felonious assault.

U visas mirror T visas, with some exceptions. T visa applicants must apply in the U.S. U visa applicants can apply from in or outside the U.S. T visa applicants must prove extreme hardship if removed from the U.S. U visa applicants must show substantial physical or mental abuse as a result of the crime. At present T visas are immediately available upon approval of the application, whereas there is currently a two-year wait for U visas. U visa holders must wait three years to apply for a green card; T visa holders can apply sooner than three years if the criminal case concludes. T visa holders can include more family members in their applications. U visas do not trigger federal public benefits.

What is the role of immigration attorneys in the collaborative work to serve survivors of human trafficking?

Immigration attorneys can screen, or jointly screen with one or more attorneys, not only for immigration relief, but also for wage and hour, family, housing, and other civil legal remedies. If survivors have basic needs (food, clothing, shelter), immigration attorneys should know to whom and how best to refer survivors for services. In states such as California, immigration attorneys can provide letters acknowledging representation on a T visa, thus allowing survivors to seek state public benefits.

If the trafficking case has not been already identified by law enforcement, immigration attorneys can determine with survivors whether and how to report the trafficking. Promising practices recommend conducting law enforcement interviews of trafficking survivors in a familiar setting, such as the attorney's office or victim services' office. Reports of trafficking can also be made to the Department of Labor, which can issue certifications of cooperation for T and U visas.

Each agency/person involved in investigations and in survivor services should provide a personal handoff to the other, so survivors know the other agency/person can be trusted. While each agency has its own role to play and responsibilities, all agencies interacting with a survivor should be working in tandem so that information provided to the survivor is consistent, no promises are made that cannot be fulfilled, and every effort is made to minimize re-traumatizing the survivor.

43 - What is the difference between a victim and a survivor?

The answer to this question may appear to be a simple point of semantics, but it isn't. While the terms can be used interchangeably at times, the distinction is important.

The word "victim" is commonly used within law enforcement, and even VSPs, to describe the victim of a criminal act. The term has legal implications since being labeled a "victim" grants reliefs and benefits to victims of crime.

The term "survivor" has become more prevalent over the past several years, and rightly so. This term implies respect for the survivor's strength and courage to move through—and hopefully past—their experience and is not limited to human trafficking: There are survivors of sexual assault, domestic violence, and other crimes. Survivors make up an important sector in the response to trafficking.

When referring to a person who has experienced modern slavery, refer to them as a survivor, for that is truly what they are.

44 - What is the role of a survivor in the response to human trafficking?

Guest Contributor: Shamere McKenzie

Shamere McKenzie is the CEO of the Sun Gate Foundation. As a survivor of human trafficking, she uses her experience in a variety of ways, including training law enforcement on how to identify and respond to victims of trafficking, informing policy-makers, and providing support to organizations working against human trafficking. She lectures both within the United States and internationally.

It takes a collaborative approach to effectively fight against human trafficking. Whether your approach is a political, a criminal justice, or a human rights response, it is important that survivors of human trafficking are involved. Survivors of human trafficking are key players and must be at the forefront of this fight.

Respect of Choice and Freedom

It is important to understand that not all survivors will want to join the fight. Some survivors may choose to utilize their freedom to pursue their own dreams. This may include a dream to be a doctor or lawyer, to return to school, or to pursue another opportunity. Some survivors may choose not to disclose their experience and just want to live their lives in their own way. While in captivity, many survivors were denied the privilege of choice. Therefore, one major way to empower survivors is to respect their choice and freedom. Allow survivors to maximize their freedom and live the life they imagine.

Each Survivor Experience is Unique

Rachel Lloyd, Founder, CEO of Girls Educational and Mentoring Service (GEMS) and survivor, often states that survivors are not a monolithic group. Each survivor has a unique experience that may impact the role they play in the response to human trafficking. In addition, each survivor's individual perspective may impact the way they view the issue as a whole. Therefore, it is important to understand that survivors may have differing opinions regarding various aspects of trafficking.

More Than a Story

While survivor stories are important, they must be utilized properly, and survivors must be seen as more than a story. Therefore, when considering inviting a survivor to participate in an event, be sure to clearly outline the purpose. If it is merely to share their story, then reconsider your purpose and invitation. Understand that each survivor's story is a delicate and intimate part of their life. Thus, their stories should be treated as such, rather than as vehicles for placating someone's desire to hear a sad experience or story. One way to ensure that you are inviting the survivor story in a beneficial way is to ask the question, "How will sharing his or her story empower or benefit this survivor?" Organizations are often tempted to invite a survivor to speak at their event for the sole purpose of sharing their story. Some may even justify their actions through compensation. There is no compensation enough for a survivor to share their deepest, darkest moments with an audience simply to tell a story. If you think there is, then you should ask yourself whether you are involved in exploitation: giving a story for money, giving a body for money. As you can see, money is the common denominator.

Survivors at the Center

There are many ways in which survivors can effectively utilize their voices.

- **Education/Awareness**
  Survivor's voices can be used to spread awareness and educate the public on what human trafficking looks like in various communities. Survivors can play an important role in many ways, including:
  - Writing/revising curriculums for schools, programs, etc.,

- Designing and implementing public awareness campaigns, and
- Developing and delivering training to various professionals.

- **Consulting**

  Everyone is eager to make a difference and join the fight. However, what one may consider a great idea may not necessarily be the best solution. Therefore, survivors can serve a critical role in evaluating what works and what does not work by, for example:

  - Providing recommendations on how programs can best meet the needs of survivors, and
  - Using their experience to advise on policy.

- **Mentoring/Advocating**

  Restoration is an ongoing process, and therefore, survivors need adequate support from individuals who understand their situation. Who best provides this support than survivors themselves who have already walked the path? This support can take many forms, such as

  - Mentoring other survivors of human trafficking, and
  - Advocating for effective treatment and services.

A Message to Survivors

If, as a survivor, you choose to get involved in the fight against human trafficking, there are a couple of things you should understand.

- There is no rush. Take ample time to work on your healing and to find your place in the movement.
- Your story is your intellectual property; you own it and have the power to decide when and how to use it.
- You need to be able to bring more than just your experience to the table. Therefore, take the necessary steps to address your personal and professional development. Rebecca Bender, founder, Executive Director of Rebecca

Bender Ministries and survivor states, "Living through a fire doesn't make you an arson expert." To prepare for future opportunities, consider getting educated in the area you want to be involved in. In addition, consider formal training in public speaking, policy, or human services. These types of preparation will position you more effectively for future service.

- You are a valuable stakeholder similar to those in law enforcement, policy-making, victim services, etc. and therefore, should be treated as such.

CHAPTER 5

Responding to Human Trafficking: Law Enforcement Challenges

Willingly no one chooses the yoke of slavery.
AESCHYLUS, AGAMEMNON

Both federal and local law enforcement agencies participate in the investigation and prosecution of trafficking incidents. But not every agency is equally prepared for the task, and many challenges will take years to overcome. Accepting that trafficking occurs within the community, cultivating awareness, providing investigative training, and allowing time for collaborative engagement can start now and will go a long way toward strengthening law enforcement's response to trafficking incidents.

45 - What are the challenges faced by law enforcement leaders?

Guest Contributor: Derek Marsh
Dep. Chief (ret.) Derek Marsh is the current Bureau of Justice Assistance (BJA) Visiting Fellow in Human Trafficking, which involves researching, developing, and presenting training and technical support for human trafficking task forces in labor trafficking. After 26 years of service, Derek retired from the Westminster (CA) Police Department where he co-chaired the Orange County Human Trafficking Task Force from 2004-2012. Derek teaches an undergraduate human trafficking course at Vanguard University, in Costa Mesa, CA.

Law enforcement leadership is essential for anti-human trafficking task forces. Federal, state, local, and tribal law enforcement executives lead by providing resources, developing strategic goals, and initiating collaborations with VSPs, NGOs, FBOs and other groups and individuals who want to impact human trafficking. Law enforcement managers and supervisors develop strategies and tactics to implement those goals, leverage the available resources, and participate in collaborations. Law enforcement supervisors, line level officers, and support staff generate actionable intelligence, pursue investigations, assist in liberating victims from their captors, and sustain coalitions and collaborations by building and maintaining professional relationships with multi-jurisdictional task force members.

Unfortunately, most law enforcement personnel do not wake up one day and decide they are going to start or participate in an anti-trafficking task force, develop and pursue investigations, collaborate with a variety of VSPs, NGOs, FBOs to eliminate human trafficking, and help release victims from their captivity so they can begin the journey of survivorship. In this section, I hope to address some of the challenges law enforcement faces with regards to effectively participating in and sustaining anti-human trafficking investigations in collaboration with a task force.

Fair warning: My experience as a local law enforcement officer for more than 26 years has led me to view many issues from that perspective. The issues discussed below are taken from my experience and from the experiences of the many dedicated law enforcement officers—federal, state, local and tribal—as well as the dedicated VSPs, NGOs, FBOs, MANGOs and volunteers with whom I have had the honor of collaborating while engaged in anti-human trafficking activities.

Does a task force more effectively address the crime of human trafficking?

Yes. I first became involved in anti-human trafficking investigations at the local level starting in 2004. Our first case, more luck than intent, found two Thai women who were potential trafficking victims. I had great confidence in my officers' and supervisors' ability to handle any variety of investigations. I was aware of the "need" for collaboration, but a part of me still felt we could succeed independently. I kept a couple of VSPs in the loop as this first potential trafficking case progressed, just to be polite, but kept them at arm's length.

I won't say we did a poor job, but we could have done much better. We immediately recognized we were in over our heads. Language barriers, immigration issues, food-clothing-shelter for the victims, initial interviews with the potential victims—all became problematic in different ways and demanded expertise and resources we did not know how to access. I was glad I had kept the couple of VSPs generally aware of our investigation. We called for assistance; they responded quickly and professionally handled the issues we were not prepared to confront.

We learned our lesson swiftly: Human trafficking is a team effort.

How do we get law enforcement engaged in anti-trafficking efforts?

The answer depends on the type of law enforcement you are trying to get to participate, and the question itself has become more of a moot point in the past few years.

Federal law enforcement (Dept. of Homeland Security, Federal Bureau of Investigation, the Department of Labor) and prosecutors (Assistant United States Attorneys) have mandates to investigate and prosecute human trafficking cases. For instance, the National Human Trafficking Hotline (888-373-7888), run by the Polaris Project, takes tips from around the country regarding potential human trafficking incidents. When the hotline gets a viable tip, they send it to the local task force (if there is one), to the FBI, and to DHS. The FBI, DHS and AUSAs each have personnel committed to anti-human trafficking efforts, including both enforcement and victim support.

State, local, and tribal law enforcement engagement can be more problematic. Prior to 2010 when the federal government created the Enhanced Collaborative Model Human Trafficking

Task Force program and encouraged funded task forces to pursue Domestic Minor Sex Trafficking (DMST), getting law enforcement to actively participate in anti-human trafficking efforts focused on convincing executive leadership that a predominantly international crime (again, the perception at the time) had local relevance. To garner support for the global crime nexus to local criminal activities, you would have to address the fact that some of the victims were in the United States illegally. Their illegal status, at least in California and many border states, was frequently conflated with illegal immigration issues and attitudes. In short, the decision to participate in anti-human trafficking efforts was an ongoing and politically charged issue before 2010. In some cases, this confusion remains today.

Since 2010 and the reaffirmation of DMST, many state, local, and tribal law enforcement leaders have been much more willing to pursue anti-human trafficking investigations and collaborations. What law enforcement leader wants to be perceived as not actively supporting investigations, prosecutions, and collaborations addressing local teenagers being repeatedly sexually exploited?

What is the predominant challenge facing law enforcement when pursuing human trafficking cases?

Mindset. Law enforcement officers are trained from Day One of the police academy to become creatures of habit.

This is not intended as a criticism. Many of the habits we begin to learn in the academy save the lives of both officers and citizens. These include arrest and control techniques, weapons practice, tactical deployment strategies and tactics (generally, and for specific types of incidents), how to effectively drive a vehicle, and the investigative process. All of this training creates habits that contribute to our survival.

However, these set patterns of behavior do not always prepare officers for new concepts or processes such as those required for investigating human trafficking, collaborating with multiple stakeholders, and providing support and resources to survivors.

Many officers do not understand what the crime of human trafficking entails. When they learn about it, they often focus on sex trafficking, as it is closest to crimes with which they are familiar like child sexual assault, rape, and prostitution. It is difficult for many officers to process a victim-centered, trauma-informed approach to investigations, a procedure distinctly different from the one followed when finding a criminal act, arresting the suspects, interviewing the victims and witnesses, and then moving on to the next case. I do not mean to state or imply law enforcement officers are not compassionate to victims; instead, it is important to realize that once a victim has been interviewed and referred to a victim services provider, in most cases the investigator then shifts the focus to gathering the evidence required to prosecute the suspects.

Associating multiple types of crimes with human trafficking is accurate; however, officers tend to believe the same independent investigative process applies to all of these crimes because this technique has worked in the past. As I mentioned earlier with regards to my team's first case of trafficking, this mindset of handling a trafficking case on our own was counterproductive. I have always considered myself open-minded and willing to adopt new changes; however, my behavior during that first case was a personal epiphany of sorts about how mindset can influence both one's behaviors and another's *perception of those behaviors*. I told myself I was breaking new investigative ground. Instead, I found I was applying old habits to a new and much more complex collaborative issue.

What is the predominant challenge facing law enforcement involved in human trafficking collaborations?

In short, training law enforcement officers to appreciate the mindset and practices of victim service providers and other non-law enforcement stakeholders and to work cooperatively with them has proved to be both an ongoing challenge—and a promising opportunity.

Law enforcement personnel collaborate well and in fact have extensive histories of collaboration—with other law enforcement agencies. In the 1980's and 1990's the guiding philosophies in law enforcement included community-oriented policing and problem-oriented policing. In the late 1990's and 2000's, our country's war on terror focused on local and federal collaborations and introduced intelligence-led policing and fusion centers. We created county or parish task forces focused on drug crimes, criminal street gangs, and vehicle theft—just to name a few. All of these actions have continued to serve their varied purposes. However, they involve teams composed predominantly of law enforcement officers from diverse agencies.

Anti-human trafficking task forces require a significantly wider range of participants, and those participants are not predominantly law enforcement. Remember, the trauma-informed, victim-centered approach necessitates VSPs, NGOs, FBOs, MANGOs and volunteers to all participate and provide their skills and expertise to comprehensively address human trafficking issues and support survivors. If you look at the 4P Paradigm discussed in Chapter 3, law enforcement has traditionally focused almost exclusively on "Protection" through investigations, identifying victims, and arresting traffickers.

All of the participating agencies and organizations are working together towards the goal of eliminating trafficking. However, many of them use different methods and techniques to reach that goal. These differences necessarily bring agencies into potential conflict over how to complete their respective tasks. I have attended many task force meetings and conferences in the past 11 years. At each event I have seen and heard the same issue time and time again expressed by both law enforcement and VSPs, from both new and established task force stakeholders: "They don't get us and what we need to do," followed quickly by, "Why do they do it *that* way?" There is no easy answer for these questions because they require bridging individual and agency mindsets and values.

However, the challenges faced by task forces also bring an opportunity—an opportunity to bring respect for other views to the table, to value the good intentions of all parties, and to build trust over time through successful collaboration. While each actor must adhere to the mandates of his or her agency, each also needs to understand that they may not always see issues in the same way and must be willing to establish and maintain an open dialogue regarding perceptions and misperceptions. In addition, task force members must stay up-to-date on best practices, changing laws, and task force roles and expectations. The most successful task forces with which I have worked were not the most successful because of their statistics: They were successful because of their mutual respect and positive, open communications with a wide scope of agencies and organizations.

46 - Why are human trafficking cases difficult to identify and prosecute?

For a variety of reasons, human trafficking cases are more difficult to identify than other crime types. Here are some of the most common barriers.

Lack of human trafficking awareness spans every segment of society, including victims. Most victims of trafficking don't attach the term *human trafficking* to their own victimization, so they rarely self-identify as a trafficking victim. I know of only one case where a victim walked into a police station and announced, "I'm a victim of human trafficking, and I want to file a report." And in this particular situation, the victim had already met with an attorney who told the victim exactly what to do and say. Victims usually don't know about human trafficking, just as most people in general don't know about human trafficking.

When victims do report being victimized, they usually report a different type of crime; they say they were "forced into prostitution" or "forced to work" against their will. They may say they were threatened with physical violence or actually assaulted, but they are reporting as victims of assault, not trafficking.

Why is this lack of self-identification important? Because if a crime is not reported, there is no record of its occurrence; it doesn't exist in the quantitative sense.

Most often, the response to any criminal activity begins with someone reporting a crime, usually by dialing 911. Most local police officers and sheriff's deputies perform what is referred to as "reactive policing"; they react to a reported crime. (While federal agencies such as the Federal Bureau of Investigation [FBI] and Homeland Security Investigation/Immigration and Customs Enforcement [HSI/ICE] also conduct human trafficking investigations, most victims of crime contact local law enforcement agencies to report their victimization.) Lack of reporting is a fundamental reason for this common statement by police leadership: "We don't have human trafficking in our community."

In addition to the lack of human trafficking awareness among its victims, police officers and detectives also fail to recognize trafficking—usually due to inadequate training on the topic. If a victim reports being "forced into prostitution," but the officer taking the report or investigating the case doesn't know the difference between prostitution and trafficking, the case may never get examined as a case of human trafficking. Even greater difficulty can be found in identifying cases of labor trafficking, as most law enforcement officers never receive any training on labor law or violations of wage and hour employment regulations.

Training officers and detectives is both time consuming and expensive for law enforcement agencies, even if the training takes only an hour or two. Many states mandate training on specific topics (such as use of force, weapons or driver training, and updates on CPR and First Aid), leaving agencies with little time to train their officers on new emerging topics such as trafficking. Consider this: If victims don't report being trafficking victims and the police don't know how to recognize trafficking incidents, then few—if any—cases are identified, leading police leadership to believe trafficking is not occurring in the community. So why *should* they train their officers?

Mandated training sounds like the answer, but how "mandated" training is enforced must be considered when weighing this option. For example, in 2012, the California human trafficking law was modified to include a provision that "Every law enforcement officer who is assigned field or investigative duties shall complete a minimum of two hours training ... by July 1, 2014, or within six months of being assigned to that position, whichever is later." The intent of this provision should be applauded. But because the mandate did not include a specific penalty on agencies for not providing this training, the majority of officers in California still have not received two hours of training on human trafficking, despite a variety of efforts to create and disseminate training tools to law enforcement agencies.

Abolitionists hoping to mandate training and awareness (at least at the state level) should keep this example in mind.

While it is critical for law enforcement officers to understand human trafficking, it is just as important that victim advocates and VSPs also receive training on how to recognize potential trafficking victims. Often, victims of sexual assault or domestic violence initially reach out to shelters or crisis centers for help, and advocates help the victims report the crimes to police. By learning to recognize human trafficking, advocates and service providers can help victims more accurately report these crimes.

Finally, the critical role of the local prosecutor's office must be examined. Prosecutors (and public defenders) knowledgeable on trafficking may identify an incident the investigating detective failed to recognize. In addition, prosecutors who have received training specifically on trafficking laws and prosecution tactics will be more likely to charge offenders using trafficking statutes—as opposed to using other criminal statutes. If prosecutors charge offenders under a trafficking statute, offenders will be found guilty of trafficking, confirming the existence of human trafficking in the community.

In all fairness, when deciding what statutes to charge in any criminal case, prosecutors must consider the knowledge base of the potential jury and strategically choose statutes likely to return a successful conviction. The perspective of the jury members and the importance the community places on responding to human trafficking also impact the decisions the prosecutor will make. The role of the jury provides one more reason for increasing public awareness of human trafficking: An educated public brings basic knowledge to the jury pool.

These are the core reasons trafficking incidents are hard to identify, prosecute, and ultimately, count as human trafficking cases and trafficking-related convictions. The old chicken and egg analogy applies here: If trafficking cases are not identified, then they must not be occurring, which means we don't need to provide training to investigators and prosecutors (without which they will not identify cases), which in turn perpetuates the belief that trafficking is not occurring in the community.

Of course this isn't the case. Trafficking can occur anywhere. If law enforcement is not finding trafficking in the community, law enforcement is probably not looking for trafficking in the community.

47 - Which police units are best poised to investigate human trafficking?

Guest Contributor: Jon A. Daggy
Detective Sergeant Jon Daggy is an investigator and supervisor with the Human Trafficking Vice Unit of the Indianapolis Metropolitan Police Department.

Does it matter which unit within a police department investigates human trafficking? Or is the perspective of the individual investigators in that unit more important?

Law enforcement agencies name their specialized units for a variety of reasons, including tradition and the type of work performed. Traditional names include the Homicide Unit, the Sexual Assault Unit, and the SWAT (Special Weapons and Tactics) Team. But most agencies are not large enough to have specialized units for every type of crime or enforcement activity. Unit names reflecting broader responsibilities, such as General Investigations, Detective Bureau, or Crimes against Persons (or Property) Unit, are more common.

Also, new language has been adopted by law enforcement to better describe the victims they assist or their approach to the work they do, such as a Special Victims Unit focusing on victims of sexual assault or child abuse, or the Special Operations Unit, which may use special weapons and tactics at times but might also perform undercover operations. While different police agencies have units with the same title, the exact work performed by those units can vary; the only way to know for sure exactly what types of crime a particular unit has responsibility for is to ask a member of that agency.

Though human trafficking encompasses both sex and labor exploitation, it is common for local law enforcement agencies to view the issue primarily as a commercial sex crime, which in the history and tradition of policing, falls to the responsibility of a Vice Unit. Traditionally, vice-related crimes include prostitution, gambling, alcohol licensing enforcement, and within some agencies, narcotics investigations. While some law enforcement agencies place responsibility for trafficking investigations within vice units, other agencies may not have vice units, or they have changed the name of units to reflect their recognition of human trafficking.

Indianapolis Metro Police Department (IMPD) formally changed the name of their Vice Unit to the Human Trafficking Vice Unit after receiving federal funding to create a human trafficking task force; the new name reflects a change in the focus and perspective of the unit. At the time, no other units showed a desire to investigate the crime or displayed an understanding of human trafficking as well as the vice detectives. The decision to change the unit's name was made by the supervisors within the unit but required the approval of the chief of police.

Regardless of the unit's name, the more important factor is the knowledge, perspective, and professional culture the individual officers bring to their work. When the IMPD took on the responsibility of investigating human trafficking, it required change among the detectives. When investigating prostitution cases, detectives changed the way they viewed these women; the detectives looked deeper into why the women were involved in commercial sex and who might be behind their exploitation. Traditional (and negative) terms that were used to describe these women were no longer used within the unit because genuine concern developed—even for the women and men who were not trafficking victims.

Instead of making a quick arrest of suspected "prostitutes," the detectives were trained to dig deeper in their investigations in an effort to find the trafficker. Detectives slowed the pace of their investigations and delayed their arrests as they tried to find the elements of human trafficking: force, fraud, or coercion. Every potential victim or suspect was interviewed in an effort to increase the chance of uncovering a human trafficking case. These investigations made traditional vice detectives rethink and refocus their perspectives. As a result, they felt they were making a difference and actually helping people, especially women and children. More arrests for sex trafficking-related crimes were made in a three-year span than in the prior 50 years in Indianapolis. The trafficker was now the target.

Also, because of victim services made available by the task force, there were resources and programs available for women who wanted to get out of "the life" (a street-term for prostitution or the sex trade) even if they were not identified as victims of trafficking.

It would be ideal if every police department and sheriff's office had a specialized unit devoted to investigating all forms of human trafficking. But in the absence of a Human Trafficking Unit or HEAT Unit (Human Exploitation and Trafficking—an increasingly popular name), human trafficking will be investigated by whichever unit an agency's leadership determines is best qualified—and only if that unit exists within the organization.

In any case, identifying victims of human trafficking cannot be left to any single unit. An effective response requires every agency member, from patrol operations to investigations to agency leadership, be trained to identify human trafficking incidents and to work with service providers to assist victims.

It is not the name of the investigating unit that matters; it is the trained professional with the knowledge to identify trafficking and the empathy and skills to assist victims that is most crucial in the fight against slavery and exploitation.

48 - What strategies make a human trafficking case prosecutable?

Guest Contributor: Susan French

Former Senior Special Counsel for Human Trafficking in the Human Trafficking Prosecution Unit, Criminal Section, Civil Rights Division, U.S. Department of Justice, Susan French has and continues to consult and train national and international law enforcement and civil society organizations.

Agents and non-governmental organizations are often frustrated by presenting a case that they believe factually supports a trafficking violation and merits prosecution, only to be rejected by a prosecutor. By "trafficking violation," I mean federal violations including forced labor, involuntary servitude, peonage, and document servitude, found in Title 18, United States Code, Chapter 77.[1] Trafficking is an offense against a person and is different than smuggling—an offense against a nation and its borders. Most prosecutors have limited, if any, experience developing or prosecuting trafficking cases. Human trafficking cases are victim,[2] not document and forensics, driven. Trafficking victims have been exploited and traumatized, necessitating extreme patience by prosecutors and agents. Sensitivity is essential when planning and conducting victim interviews. Victims often need time to recover from the emotional, mental, and physical harm caused by the traffickers. Victims may suppress painful experiences for self-protection, and their version of events may evolve or change over time. Prosecutors experienced in working with traumatized crime victims are better able to understand that evolving recollections and suppression of bad events can be explained and don't necessarily undermine a trafficking case since these memory patterns are commonly associated with traumatized persons. Despite these obstacles, prosecutors are public servants and should persevere and meet the challenges of developing prosecutable labor trafficking cases. Let's examine the essentials of such a case. I share what I have learned from my and other colleagues' experiences. Many of these "essentials" also apply to commercial sex trafficking cases.

First, the case must involve a credible victim(s) who can tell what happened to him/her in a courtroom of strangers. Credible victims must be truth tellers, not eloquent public speakers. A credible victim is a believable victim who can also explain what may seem to be "bad facts," "prior or subsequent inconsistent statements," or what appears to be contradictory behavior in the context of his/her experience as a trafficked person.

Prosecutors view the witnesses and evidence with an eye toward trial. The prosecutor knows she/he must prove the case "beyond a reasonable doubt," the standard in criminal cases, which does not mean beyond all doubt, but *reasonable* doubt. In criminal cases, jurors must all concur to convict. No case is perfect. Prosecutors must believe in the case or not bring it, but they should not shrink from their duty to bring justice to trafficking victims because the case is difficult, challenging, or advances the law.

Second, the victim's description of events must provide a factual basis that supports the elements of the charged offense. In forced labor trafficking cases, the most frequent missing or weak element is the unlawful coercion used by the suspects to compel the victim's labor or services. The prosecutor must prove that the suspect knowingly obtained the labor or services of a person by an unlawful (coercive) means.[3] The coercion *must* be directly linked to compelling a victim to perform labor or services and can be any or all of the following actions: (1) force or threats of force or physical restraint; (2) abuse of the law or legal process (using the law or legal process for a bad faith purpose—threatening deportation when a worker complains about not being paid or bad conditions); (3) threats of or use of "serious harm" against that person or another; and (4) a scheme or plan that makes a person believe she/he or another will suffer "serious harm"[4] if she/he does not perform the labor or services. Under the law, "serious harm" can be physical or non-physical including actual harm, psychological, financial, or reputational harm, or any and all conduct that taken in its entirety would make a similarly situated person believe he/she had no reasonable choice but to continue performing the labor or services. Coercion may be established by direct or circumstantial evidence.

Third, corroborating witnesses are important, however small the detail(s) corroborated. Each case differs. Single victim domestic servitude cases are the most challenging to corroborate because the victim typically lives in isolation in the suspect's house. Family members, friends, and neighbors may be inclined to support the suspect's family, but not always, and may provide some "insider" information. Prosecutors should subpoena witnesses to testify before the grand jury because the power of that body promotes truth telling. In one domestic servitude case, none of the defendants' closest friends knew that the victim lived in the defendants' house for 19 years, nor, had they ever heard her name—establishing her total isolation. This testimony needs to be "locked-in" before a grand jury to preserve it for trial if the witness balks. In the same case, no neighbor had ever seen the victim and so testified at trial. Moreover, the defendants' adult daughter reluctantly testified at trial about the convoluted and oppressive house rules that kept the victim out of sight for years. In another domestic servitude case, the victim's children were brought from their home country, and one testified that in over 8 years she was able to speak with her mother only once on the phone and the children had only received $300 for the victim's 8.5 years of domestic work. In two other domestic servitude cases, neighbors reported that they had seen the victims, but each victim was always in the presence of the subject/defendant and usually was working. In domestic servitude cases, prior servant victims may have similar experiences and admissible testimony.

Multiple victim cases offer an opportunity to be selective about who can better testify about events. Moreover, the case is not dependent on one victim's testimony. Typically, multiple victims can corroborate significant coercive events—defendants' threats of harm or deportation, beatings, lock-ins, food deprivations, bad living conditions, house rules limiting the free movement of victims, confiscation of documents to limit free movement, etc. People's recollections can honestly differ about the same incident. Multiple victims may contradict each other, but if the different recollection is not on a material (significant point) and relevant legal issue, prosecutors can object and explain that it is immaterial to the legal issues before the court. Also, the law does not require that every person similarly situated be a "victim" under the law to prosecute a case on behalf of some actual victims. In my first agricultural labor involuntary servitude case, we initially were confused about why 8 out of 53 possible victims were free to leave the labor camp when they wanted. As we investigated, we learned that workers with a smuggling debt were restricted in their movement. Once a worker paid off his debt, he was free to come and go at will.

Fourth, corroborating documents, physical evidence, or photographs (or their absence) can support the victim's version of events. In a domestic servitude case, the husband and wife defendants insisted that the victim was treated as family. Federal agents testified and demonstrated at trial, through a video taken during the execution of a search warrant, that no photograph of the victim was displayed in the 10,000 square foot house despite numerous family photos. In yet another domestic servitude case, an illiterate Nigerian victim entered the United States on a date she was certain of, but she had no documents to prove it. (Her documents were confiscated upon arrival, and she had never looked at them because she was instructed not to and she could not read.) Federal data bases did not show her entering the United States. A dutiful federal agent searched a U.S. Department of State data base entering combinations of known associated names and located the victim's photograph on a visa displaying the male defendant's last name and his mother's given name (named in *his* immigration file). The victim's entry date and absence of departure date was established through the U.S. Departments of State and Homeland Security records and agency employee testimony.

Search warrants can produce relevant and material evidence and documents. Each case differs, but the search may include bogus debt contracts binding victim to subject for large debts, payroll and financial records, money orders and evidence of financial transfers, letters and communications by any means (computers), confiscated documents, false admissions in writing, weapons, photographs etc. Beware of employer/defendant produced payroll records as I have seen many fabricated records. Even if a victim was given a payroll slip, question whether the victim received money when cashing checks and whether the money was in his/her account when an ATM card was used. Money disappears!

Fifth, anticipate, understand, and front (never hide) a victim's prior or subsequent inconsistent statement, benefits provided by the government to the victim, and all bias facts (evidence showing that a witness may be favorable to the government). Some prosecutors unnecessarily worry about benefits the U.S. Congress has decided to provide to trafficking victims including immigration relief, emergency cash benefits, temporary housing, medical assistance, etc. Through the victim and federal agent witnesses, the prosecutor can explain that these benefits were authorized by Congress, not the prosecutor. Presented with this information in a thoughtful way, a jury typically can be proud that this country cares about human trafficking and provides services and benefits to victims. Know that the defense will always argue that the victim(s) have fabricated the story to receive the government benefits. Savvy prosecutors will attempt to interview the victim before she/he is informed of these benefits so that the defense's argument will fail. In most cases, victims will make statements that in some way contradict another statement. Prosecutors must discuss inconsistencies with the victim and often will receive an explanation that can be embraced as part of the trafficker's scheme. Letters from and to the victim may help or undermine your case. Victims may write soothing letters to family back home so the family will not worry or because the subjects forced them to write the letter. Again, embrace and explain the purpose behind the "I am well" letters.

Sixth, anticipate the frequent and usual defenses and identify which are factual and which may be legal defenses. Prosecutors are wise to brief every unique legal issue for the court and file appropriate motions prior to, or if necessary, during trial. Common defenses include the victim is better off in the U.S. (not a legal defense); the victim initially agreed to come to the U.S. and work (not a legal defense, and no one can agree to a violation of the 13th Amendment); the victim was paid; the victim was not locked in and could have obtained help (not a legal defense if the victim reasonably believed he/she could not leave the trafficker); and the victim received benefits and lied in order to receive them.

49 - What role do criminal gangs play in human trafficking?

Criminal gangs are not only involved in human trafficking but also poised to increase their involvement.

One could argue that organized crime, like the Mafia and other international syndicates, has been involved in human trafficking for as long as it has been involved in organized prostitution, which is a very long time. Countering these organizations is primarily the responsibility of national and international law enforcement agencies, such as the FBI and Interpol. However, local gangs are becoming more involved in trafficking, and local law enforcement is typically responsible for investigating and prosecuting their criminal activity. As a result, local and federal agencies must work together closely to combat criminal gang activities tied to human trafficking.

One excellent example of a combined local and federal law enforcement response to a street gang engaging in human trafficking is the 2011 case of the Oceanside (CA) Crips. The United States Attorney's Office charged 38 individuals under a variety of statutes, including racketeering and prostitution of minors and adults. Recruitment of the victims focused on juvenile females who were runaways, often using social media tools. United States Attorney Laura E. Duffy, in announcing the case, made her perspective clear stating, "I cannot state this more emphatically: I regard the kind of prostitution involved in this case, including the trafficking of children via the Internet, social networking sites, and local businesses, as a form of modern-day slavery to which every available law enforcement resource will be applied."[5]

Why would a criminal gang whose reputation is traditionally tied to the drug trade engage in trafficking? And why should we expect more of this in the future? Three reasons: Money. Easy acquisition of the "product." Reduced risk.

The revenue generated from forced prostitution is limited only by the number of victims available to be sold, how many johns they encounter, and the price johns are willing to pay. But a key difference between the drug trade and the sex trade lies in the ease of obtaining the product to be sold. If a gang is selling cocaine, the coca must be grown, harvested, and processed (typically in South America) before being transported and smuggled into the United States. All of this entails a cost that must be factored into the final sale price and includes great risk to the drug trafficker. And of course once the drug is consumed by the buyer, the drug is gone and must be replenished by the drug dealer.

Sex traffickers do not face complicated and risky supply-chain problems. They can openly recruit potential victims on the street or via phone, text, or social media. Once obtained, their "product" is not lost the first time it is sold but can be resold over and over again.

Finally, there is far less monetary and penal risk. Anti-drug enforcement efforts have always been more robust than efforts to reduce prostitution or human trafficking. If caught, sex traffickers are more likely to be charged with pimping and pandering than trafficking statutes, and the sentencing standards for pimping are typically far less than those for drug trafficking.

Awareness of human trafficking is increasing not only among the public but also within criminal gangs. Books and websites offer sex traffickers guidance on how to recruit, control, and profit from their victims. Money, plus easier access to their product, plus less risk add up to greater opportunities for profit. In light of these trends, criminal gang involvement in human trafficking will increase.

We see the importance, again, of quality training for police, prosecutors, and front-line responders. The sale of human beings for any form of exploitation should never be viewed as a minor crime and certainly not a "victimless" crime. Stopping the exploitation must become a priority.

50 - What is demand reduction?

Within the anti-trafficking community *demand reduction* refers to reducing the demand side in the supply/demand equation of *sex trafficking*.[6] In theory, arresting the buyers of sex (or otherwise preventing the purchase from ever occurring) will reduce the demand, and traffickers who fill the supply side of the equation will have less financial incentive to engage in trafficking. Without demand, sex trafficking will be reduced or eliminated. Many anti-trafficking organizations focus on the importance of demand reduction.

Although *demand operations* most commonly include police operations focused on arresting johns, other strategies can also impact demand. These alternatives include shaming, by publicizing the names of arrested johns or sending letters to the offender's home; seizing the automobile the buyer was driving at the time of arrest, thereby increasing the financial penalty (and potential for embarrassment) by having to pay impound and towing fees; suspension of the arrestee's driver's license; restraining orders issued to johns (or suspected johns) prohibiting them from being in areas of known prostitution, commonly called SOAP orders, an acronym for Stay Out of Areas with Prostitution; public awareness programs; and john schools.

In a 2012 report funded by the U.S. Department of Justice, *A National Overview of Prostitution and Sex Trafficking Demand Reduction Efforts*,[7] researchers extensively examined these strategies. They concluded some strategies offered promising outcomes, but not enough of these strategies were deployed at the time to determine concrete results, stating, "It is premature to make broad conclusions about the value of most tactics or program models." Readers with an interest in demand strategies are encouraged to examine this report.

Among the most popular of these strategies is the "john school." Similar to traffic school, an arrested john can attend the school in lieu of a jail sentence or criminal fine. Schools vary in this regard, but all seek to reframe the johns' perspective on buying sex by educating them about the exploitation of sex trafficking victims, the health risks involved, and the potential legal consequences of this crime. Long-running john schools point to their success reducing the recidivism rate of attendees; it appears johns who attend these programs may have a lower likelihood of buying sex in the future.

In addition, outreach programs that address human trafficking, the victimization of those forced into the sex trade, and reframing the public's perception of the sex transaction from a "victimless crime" to one of exploitation may have a role in reducing demand, though empirical evidence is limited. As with so many aspects of the response to modern slavery, more research is needed. But that does not mean we shouldn't make the effort now. Developing programs that address how young men view women and what those men think about purchasing sex, along with programs for young women that expose the realities of the sex trade, might help change a common perception among today's youth that engaging in commercial sex is just part of life, even "cool." The reality is that it dehumanizes everyone involved.

Law enforcement primarily conducts two types of antitrafficking operations, and it is important to understand the differences between them.

Demand operations focus on arresting johns by using one of two tactics. When focusing on street-level sex trafficking, police officers (usually, but not always, women) go undercover and walk the street appearing to be available for purchase. If working an online sting, officers post ads purporting to sell sex and lure the johns to a location (usually a hotel) where the arrest will be made. With a staff of 8-10 officers, these operations can lead to the arrest of many buyers in a short amount of time, perhaps 15-20 arrests over the course of an eight-hour work shift, because the buyers can be scheduled to arrive every 30 or 45 minutes. These types of operations can be very popular with police administrators because they can report a high number of arrests. In addition, there is a leveraging effect if the arrestees are denounced in public as part of a broader shaming campaign.

Anti-trafficking operations, on the other hand, target the trafficker. They are more complex, take more time, and lead to fewer arrests for the same amount of time invested. Officers begin by examining websites advertising sex for sale. The officer phones the number listed in the ad and portrays himself as a john looking for "out call" service, where the woman comes to the man's location, usually a hotel. Once the appointment is made, officers set-up surveillance outside the hotel looking for the woman to arrive, hopefully in the company of her trafficker. The woman is arrested when she enters the room of the undercover officer while other officers arrest the trafficker.

In the best outcome, the woman tells the police she is forced by her trafficker to engage in commercial sex. She is then treated as a victim and given access to VSPs who will assist her. Meanwhile, the trafficker is booked on charges of human trafficking.

These operations must be performed one at a time, thus limiting the number of potential arrests during the course of the work shift, and also require 8-10 officers to properly and safely conduct. With luck, perhaps one or two trafficking victims will be identified, and their traffickers will go to jail.

While demand operations can arrest a lot of buyers in a short time, anti-trafficking operations offer the possibility of identifying actual victims of trafficking. Both types of operations are needed in a comprehensive law enforcement response, but to perform demand operations only is to leave victims unidentified and unassisted.

Both the demand and anti-trafficking operations described focus only on commercial sex trafficking and have no impact on labor trafficking. When communities cry out for police action against trafficking, it is tempting for law enforcement agencies to see sex trafficking as the only form of trafficking. And that, of course, is incorrect.

CHAPTER 6

Be an Abolitionist: Your Role in Combating Human Trafficking

Act as if what you do makes a difference. It does.
WILLIAM JAMES

Anyone can take part in the response to human trafficking. The topics addressed in this chapter are relevant to those who have a professional role, desire a professional role, or seek to become involved as part of a community response.

51 - What is a modern-day abolitionist?

As used in this book, the term *abolitionist* refers to someone who opposes slavery, nothing more, nothing less. But some people link the term with other meanings.

Often associated with the American Civil War and efforts to free the slaves, the term *abolitionist* is just as valid today as it was 160 years ago. During the American debate on slavery in the decades leading to the Civil War, many abolitionists used Christian values and Bible verses to support their stance. At the same time, there were other self-described abolitionists who based their arguments against slavery on constitutional or moral grounds, without invoking religious beliefs. These secular and spiritual abolitionists both fought to end slavery, just as they do today.[1]

To be a modern-day abolitionist means understanding the complexity of modern slavery and being willing to take a role in the fight for freedom. That role need not be a full-time job or even a part-time passion; it can be as simple as being aware that human trafficking occurs, that it may be occurring in your community, and that you support public and private efforts to assist victims and prosecute traffickers. It also means you share your interest and knowledge on the subject.

My definition is this: The modern abolitionist opposes all forms of slavery and seeks to assist all types of victims, regardless of gender, age, nationality, ethnicity, religion, or sexual orientation. Abolitionists place equal value and effort on every victim and on prosecuting every case possible.

To stand for freedom and oppose slavery makes you an abolitionist.

52 - How do global supply chains, human trafficking, and consumer awareness connect?

Guest Contributor: Benjamin Thomas Greer
Benjamin Thomas Greer is currently the Senior Executive on Legal Issues for the Paragon Team. The Paragon Team's mission is to help governments advance their anti-trafficking response through law enforcement training and intelligence gathering.

> *[t]he blood, sweat and tears of trafficking victims*
> *are on the hands of consumers all over the world.*
> ANTONIO M. COSTA, EXECUTIVE DIRECTOR
> UNITED NATIONS OFFICE ON DRUGS AND CRIME

Trafficking is a highly dynamic and fluid phenomenon that re-acts remarkably well to consumer demand and under-regulated economic sectors and easily adapts to exploit weaknesses in the prevailing laws. Corporate globalization of storefronts and man-ufacturing has contributed to human trafficking becoming the fastest growing and one of the most widespread criminal enter-prises in the world. The globalization of the marketplace has led to more opaque and complex supply chains. Forced labor may occur at any point through a product's life cycle—from harvesting or mining raw materials and assembling the end product to trans-porting or selling the good. Across the world, there are hundreds of thousands of trafficked people forced to work in controlled environments where the worker can be effectively isolated and dominated: remote farms, mineral quarries, raw material mines, off-shore fishing platforms, and industrial sweatshops.

Traditionally, law enforcement has employed a myopic view of human trafficking focusing primarily on the sexual exploita-tion trade (i.e., forced prostitution); however, federal and state governments, strongly influenced by advocacy groups, have begun to re-conceptualize their understanding of human traf-ficking to include the subjugation of people into forced labor.

According to the ILO's 2012 report, there are at least 21 million adults and children in forced labor, bonded labor, and forced prostitution worldwide. A 2011 U.S. Department of Labor study found 130 products from 71 countries were made by forced and child labor—most originating in Asia, Africa, and South America. With California's economy a sought-after marketplace, the state legislature wanted to increase consumer awareness through disclosures upon which societal pressures could be placed upon the retail sellers. Titled the *California Transparency in Supply Chains Act of 2010*, this law was the first to require large retail sellers to conspicuously disclose on their public website their policies, if any, to detect and fight slave labor.

While a majority of multi-national corporations do not publicly condone human trafficking, they do, however, share a common goal of maximizing profits. Lower labor costs permit companies to produce cheaper commodities, in-turn increasing their market share and profit margins. Since profits are a derivative of marketplace price and consumer demand, linking human trafficking awareness and the fair trade movement to the marketing of goods provides the required incentive to ensure complete corporate awareness. The fair trade movement seeks to promote greater equity in international trading partnerships through transparency. It promotes sustainable development by offering better working conditions to and securing the rights of marginalized workers in developing countries.

Forced labor underpins numerous global industries. From the more traditional fashion, agricultural, and mining industries, slave labor has spread to support the emerging industrial base of technology manufacturing. A vast majority of companies want to be good corporate citizens. Proper supply chain disclosures could provide an opportunity to burnish a company's brand. Numerous large companies, such as GAP, Nike, and Ford Motor Company, have already learned how impactful consumer activism can be. At one point in time, Nike was almost synonymous with slave child labor. These companies have embraced their second chance and have already posted extensive supply chain disclosures on their websites. Where industry has demonstrated a reluctance to ensure socially responsible activity, methods that utilize market forces to pressure companies ought to be advanced. Globalization of the manufacturing base and marketplace storefront encourages the movement of people and capital across borders. Because of this ubiquity, slave labor should not be considered a "niche" market phenomenon that would be hard to identify and quantify. Eradicating slavery from the global economy requires dedicated and coordinated efforts from the primary stakeholders: corporations; local, state, and federal governments; and informed consumers.

While globalization of the supply chain is not inherently predatory, trafficking syndicates often capitalize on the permeable nature of borders and the marketplaces' unique need of a large and available workforce. As corporations continue to lengthen their supply chains, searching for cheaper labor costs while utilizing technology to sell and transport goods, the risk to vulnerable populations rises. The further the supply chain is removed from the end consumer, the higher the likelihood of illicit criminal activity and the less likely the end consumer will be aware of it. A comprehensive approach to fighting trafficking involves a strong criminal justice response holding perpetrators accountable, but it also necessitates effective methods of public awareness of sourced goods to prevent future predation. As legislatures continue to formulate and structure the necessary and required responses to protect those who are vulnerable, a comprehensive "smart on crime approach" includes meaningful consumer awareness of slave-made goods.

53 - How do you create policy for the anti-trafficking movement that leads to real change?

Guest Contributor: Stephanie Kay Richard
Stephanie Kay Richard, Esq., is the Policy & Legal Services Director at the Coalition to Abolish Slavery & Trafficking (CAST) where she provides direct legal services to survivors of human trafficking and technical consultation on human trafficking cases nationwide.

Many individuals who learn about the issue of modern-day slavery are inspired to take steps to enact change in their community at the state and/or the national level. This is the type of energy and drive we need if we hope to end modern slavery in our lifetimes. However, poorly thought out and quickly drafted legislation can have unintended consequences or worse, harm the community we are hoping to assist. It can also drain political energy and will to tackle the harder or more complex changes that are often required to enact real change in the anti-trafficking movement. The responses below provide answers to questions commonly asked by those seeking policy changes in the anti-trafficking movement.

What steps should I take when I want to consider enacting legislative change in the anti-trafficking movement?

1. Talk to local, state, national, and international experts on human trafficking. They are the organizations and people working on the ground that have likely identified problems they are facing but do not have the time or capacity to work toward legislative changes. Working to create a policy change that has been identified by an individual or organization working in the field is likely to lead to enacting legislation that will have more impact. Check with multiple organizations or individuals to make sure you have identified a pressing problem or issue in the anti-trafficking movement.

2. Remember that modern slavery addresses all forms of trafficking—sex and labor; U.S. citizens and foreign nationals; men, women, and children. Oftentimes proposed legislation will seek to prevent, prosecute traffickers, or assist victims from only one subcategory of human trafficking. Ask yourself if your proposed legislative strategy can help all types of trafficking victims. If it can, make sure your proposed legislative language or any legislation you support includes protections for all types of victims. Be vocal if you find that your community or state is focusing on only one type of trafficking—as this means that many other victims will remain unidentified and enslaved for longer.

3. Make sure to vet and understand the legislative impact of your proposed solution or any legislation you support. Make sure to think about the unintended consequences or negative impacts that can result.

4. The anti-trafficking framework developed already in the Trafficking Victims Protection Act of 2000 and subsequent reauthorizations is already robust. Make sure any legislation you work on at the state or national level does not duplicate other measures that have been enacted previously.

5. Make sure your proposed change has the resources needed attached or worked into the legislative proposal. Real change usually requires expending additional resources. If your legislative enactment does not have the appropriate resources attached, it will fail to be properly implemented or worse yet, could have the unintended consequence of taking money designated to assist one vulnerable population to assist another.

6. Real change comes from not just enacting legislation but also making sure the legislation on the books is being properly implemented. Consider working on implementing legislation instead of enacting a completely new policy.

Based on my 10 years of experience working in the anti-trafficking movement, my rule of thumb is that real legislative change that has the ability to significantly impact the anti-trafficking movement is hard to establish and must address root causes and bring new resources to the issue. This means that legislative proposals can take years to enact. Don't look for simple quick solutions, but join the movement long-term and expect real change to be enacted slowly! It can take two, three, or even five to seven years for change to happen.

What steps can I take to ensure that anti-trafficking legislation is effectively implemented?

1. At the local, state and federal level, understand the legislative framework for addressing trafficking that is already enacted.
2. Identify a key issue of legislation that you think will impact real change in the anti-trafficking movement based on the criteria described above and take steps to make sure this provision is effectively implemented and resourced.
3. Map the appropriate agency targets at the state and federal level responsible for enacting this policy. At the federal level agencies as diverse as (1) Department of State, (2) Department of Health and Human Services, (3) Department of Justice, (4) Department of Labor, (5) Department of Defense, (6) Department of Education, and (7) Department of Homeland Security—as well as many others—might be essential in implementing anti-trafficking policies. Figure out who your key agency target is and identify the individuals directly responsible for enacting the provision you are targeting.
4. Conduct key outreach to ensure that your target provision has (1) effective implementing regulations or guidance, (2) is properly resourced, (3) has key staff assigned for long-term impact, and (4) if relevant, has proper agency enforcement.

What resources can I use to better educate myself about policy in the anti-trafficking movement?

Two national anti-trafficking coalitions—the Freedom Network, USA and The Alliance to End Slavery and Trafficking (ATEST)—have great resource pages explaining their policy positions and goals. These groups focus on policy changes to end all forms of human trafficking at the national level.

- Freedom Network, USA: http://freedomnetworkusa.org/about-us/policy-advocacy/
- Alliance to End Slavery & Trafficking (ATEST): https://endslaveryandtrafficking.org/policy-resources/

Polaris, which runs the National Human Trafficking Resource Center, provides a state-by-state map which shows state profiles based on hotline calls as well as summaries on a state-by-state basis of anti-trafficking legislation enacted.

- Polaris: http://www.polarisproject.org/what-we-do/policy-advocacy
- Polaris 2014 State Ratings: http://www.polarisproject.org/what-we-do/policy-advocacy/national-policy/state-ratings-on-human-trafficking-law
- National Human Trafficking Resource Center: http://traffickingresourcecenter.org/states

The Uniform Law Commission, in partnership with the American Bar Association, underwent a three-year process to create legislative recommendations for states regarding human trafficking. Of course all states are different, but asking whether your state has this basic anti-trafficking framework in place outlined by *The Uniform Act on the Prevention and Remedies for Human Trafficking* is a good start.

- Uniform Law Commission:
  http://letsendhumantrafficking.org

Finally, if you are from California or want to take action there, CAST runs a monthly policy call on legislation in California and issues action alerts. CAST policy priorities come directly from input from its own survivor advisory caucus as well as the National Survivor Network (NSN).

- Coalition to Abolish Slavery & Trafficking:
  http://www.castla.org/state-legislation
- National Survivor Network:
  http://nationalsurvivornetwork.org/

54 - What can I do to help?

I hear this question hundreds of times a year, and the answer is, "It depends."

It depends upon many factors:

- Do you seek a professional position, and if so, what type of position?
- Do you want to live in the United States or overseas?
- What is your education level or specific technical expertise?
- What traits and skills can you bring to the table?
- How much time can you commit?
- What opportunities are already available in your community?
- Do you want to create a new effort or join an existing organization?

These are just some of the considerations to weigh when exploring how to become involved. (Later, I'll describe some of the jobs available in the fight against slavery.)

But there is one opportunity that most people fail to recognize: the opportunity to be a social "connector." A connector is someone who possesses the traits and skills needed to connect one person with another. Sharing what we know about human trafficking with others expands awareness of the issue. It also helps expand the response to trafficking.

When I was part of the San Jose Police Human Trafficking Task Force, we were exploring how best to train other professions to recognize human trafficking victims. Medical staff was high on our list of professional groups we wanted to train. My wife, Dawn, is a Registered Nurse, and she gave us the idea of offering Continuing Education Units (CEUs) to RNs who attended our training. This involved completing some paperwork and paying a small fee to the State of California. But when we started to offer the training, it took us time to explain to local hospitals what our task force did, why human trafficking was an important topic for health-care professionals, and why we were offering free CEUs. (Nurses typically have to pay for CEUs and some hospital administrators questioned why we were offering them without charge.) In any case, Dawn's idea had helped us connect with a new audience, but we still faced the challenge of getting hospitals to understand why this training was important.

A few months later our task force was approached by a team of doctors from Stanford Medical Center. As part of a public health project, they wanted to train every hospital Emergency Room staff in the area on human trafficking and asked if we would partner with them on the project. This was great because by connecting with Stanford Medical Center, we overcame the challenge of how to gain access to the hospital staff; it is one thing for a police officer to phone a hospital and offer training on modern slavery, but it is quite another when a team from Stanford Medical Center is doing the calling! They connected us to more medical professionals, in much less time, than we could have accomplished ourselves. As a result of these connections, we had a very successful program.[2]

What connections can you foster through your social, professional, faith, or civic group contacts? Think about it. You probably know someone (or someone who knows someone) who would be of value to someone involved in the response to trafficking. The easiest example is offering access to a civic group. These groups are always looking for speakers, and you could connect a local expert on trafficking to your group (or give a presentation yourself). Perhaps your neighbor is the chief of police; ask her what she knows about human trafficking and help her connect with NGOs or MANGOs in the community. Your connections may also facilitate new support or donations for a local VSP.

The road to becoming a connector begins with learning about the response to human trafficking within your community and attending meetings and events. Get to know the people involved and ask them what they need. When first getting involved in anti-trafficking activities within your community, take several months to educate yourself about current efforts in your area, including any gaps that may exist, before deciding where and how to place your efforts. Sadly, too many people with great passion become disappointed and walk away often because they came in with a vision for something that was not needed at the time or because they lacked a true understanding of what was already in place. Learn what's already going on, ask others how you can help first, and then seek to create something new or fill a need—but only if it is truly needed.

Each of us can be a connector. This role may not sound exciting, but connecting others can lead to great things. Shortly after our task force delivered training to a local hospital, one of the attendees identified a patient who was a trafficking victim. The woman was safely removed from her trafficker and offered shelter by a task force VSP. At last report she was happy—and free.

55 - Which traits and abilities are valuable to an abolitionist?

Technical skills and abilities are necessary for anti-trafficking professionals, but there are traits and abilities that professionals and non-professionals alike should possess (or develop) to become effective abolitionists.

The most important trait is patience. By now you should appreciate the complexity of trafficking and the response. As a result, getting involved is like entering a marathon: There will be highs and lows, pain and joy, moments when you feel like quitting, and moments when you feel prepared to go forever. Abolitionists need patience in order to handle the slow progress as we coax communities to recognize the prevalence of trafficking and to build response capabilities. Patience is also required as new abolitionists begin to work with people already involved. Some on the front lines may be overburdened by their own efforts or unwilling to share information or knowledge. Patience with both individuals and their institutions is an important trait to possess.

Being a good listener and having the ability to learn from others is also valuable. In multidisciplinary work, it is vital to understand the other disciplines involved—but not necessarily from a technical standpoint. For example, as a police officer, I didn't need to understand the technical aspects of immigration law, but I did need to understand how immigration law could impact a victim, particularly in relation to my role in assisting our task force immigration attorney. By listening and asking questions, I not only learned about the immigration relief available to victims but also built valuable rapport and a friendship with this attorney, Lynette Parker, a contributor to this book.

Listening will also help you gain a better understanding of institutional and personal dynamics while also helping you navigate the sometimes choppy waters of collaboration.

Be humble. You may bring much to the table but probably not as much as is already at the table. Humility also helps you listen because truly humble people have a modest estimate of their own knowledge and are thus more likely to appreciate what others have to offer.

Public speaking skills help the abolitionist explain human trafficking to others. Many of the professional organizations involved in the response to trafficking cannot meet the demand for speakers on this topic. If you enjoy speaking in public, this could be an opportunity for you to forward the cause. If you are part of a task force, it is important that the task force collaborate to develop the presentation together (or at least have input from the key professional sectors) so the presentation is factual, consistent, and best reflects the work of all task force members.

Writing, editing, graphic art, and computer skills are also valuable. Again, many of the organizations will be too busy to perform many task force functions like creating protocols, logos, handout materials, or awareness literature. This is one particular area in which a volunteer abolitionist who possesses these skills can make a valuable contribution.

Finally, whether you consider it an inherent trait or a learned skill, being a life-long learner is very valuable to the abolitionist. The complexity will never go away, and there is always more to learn about trafficking, victim issues, response strategies, and collaboration. New reports and journal articles appear monthly. Each year there are more conferences related to human trafficking, most of which are open to the public and provide good opportunities to meet other abolitionists.

There are many other traits and skills useful to an abolitionist, but these are among the most important to bring to the table. And if you come to the table, you will have the chance to participate in profoundly satisfying work: fighting slavery.

56 - "We don't have human trafficking in our community." How do you respond?

I'm not sure which I hear more often: the statement that trafficking doesn't occur in a community or the question about how to respond.

We now understand many of the factors giving some people the impression trafficking does not occur in their community. Lack of victim self-identification, poor mechanisms for collecting data on victims and incidents, lack of police or prosecutor knowledge, and other factors can all play a role. So how do you reply to this statement?

The best (and first) response should be citing accurate data about cases identified within your community. Keep in mind, just because a VSP is helping trafficking victims or a MANGO is active within the community, there is no guarantee everyone else is aware of their activity. The local police chief may not be aware of these efforts. Knowledge of one or two victims in your hometown will probably resonate more deeply with community leaders than quoting the broad or unreliable estimates already discussed. Know what is happening within your community and share this information.

Second, don't limit the counting of incidents to only your town, especially if your town is relatively small; you are still connected to other towns and a larger region. Collect data on cases that have been identified in your region to illustrate that trafficking is occurring in neighboring communities. You can also look for communities across the country that mirror your community in size and demographics. If cases are being identified there, look for parallel factors in your community that could lead to trafficking.

Finally, ask the person who made this statement whether prostitution occurs in your community. If it does, explain the connection between forced prostitution and sex trafficking. I use this explanation only when I don't have data on local cases because it takes more time to explain, relies on the listener accepting that most sex workers are forced into sex exploitation, and finally, because this example focuses only on sex trafficking and doesn't touch on labor trafficking. Still, this explanation will get the point across: Human trafficking can occur in any community.

Countering those who claim trafficking doesn't exist in a community can be frustrating, so it is important to have accurate information. The bottom line is this: Human trafficking can occur within any community.

57 - How do I learn about the trafficking response in my community?

Determining the current response efforts in your community can be easy or difficult, but is the first step for an abolitionist interested in getting involved.

If you are lucky, a quick Internet search for *human trafficking task force* (or *coalition*), *human trafficking events*, or *human trafficking victim assistance* along with the name of your city or community will return websites for local organizations involved in the response. Contact them and ask to speak with the person involved in anti-trafficking work. Often, in multisector teams, this person works under the title *coordinator*. If you find an organization involved in anti-trafficking efforts they should be able to connect you with others including the local task force or coalition if one exists. Ask them what response activities are in place and how you can get involved.

For clarification, though multisector team members work closely with one another, most of the time they do not physically share the same office. Typically, team members operate from the office of their organization, and the members come together at monthly or quarterly meetings. But as anti-trafficking efforts grow, more task forces strive for the best practice of co-location, in which local and federal law enforcement officers, a trafficking victim advocate, and the task force coordinator share office space for ease of communication and coordination.

In addition to searching for local anti-trafficking organizations, connect with other members of the community. For example, if you know a local police officer or deputy, ask what they know about their agency's response to trafficking. Attending public events focusing on human trafficking and related topics is an excellent way to become involved. These events usually highlight the work of local organizations. After attending several of these events, a clear picture of the current response efforts should emerge.

Contact the National Human Trafficking Resource Center (888-373-7888) and ask if they know of organizations in your area. FBOs are also good resources for learning about local efforts.

If you cannot find any anti-trafficking efforts in your community, start one yourself! If current data doesn't exist in your community, perform an assessment. Contact all of the agencies, NGOs, and FBOs you can find and ask them whether they have served or assisted victims of trafficking. Collect as much data as you can (without asking for any personal information about the victims) with the promise to share your findings with every organization, local law enforcement, and the press. This is a great way to initiate a community response to trafficking. You can also contact the National Human Trafficking Resource Center for data on incidents they have collected and information on trafficking laws within your state.

If you cannot find local events, organize a day- or weekend-long conference. This is the best way to bring together and highlight the efforts of local organizations, which may be too busy to plan and coordinate an event.

A common error made by passionate abolitionists is launching efforts without taking the time to learn what is already in place, possibly duplicating efforts, or more likely, launching an effort before the need exists. For example, many people wish to aid victims of trafficking by opening a shelter. But for a shelter to succeed, there must be identified victims, and the agencies identifying the victims must know about the shelter and be confident in the shelter staff's background, expertise, and reliability. Forming the partnerships required to create a shelter takes incredible effort. In addition, the facility and shelter staff may have to meet certain state regulations and criteria before opening. Do the research before embarking on any endeavor, however well-intended.

In all cases, abolitionists should continue to study trafficking and response practices both within the United States and internationally; there is always more to learn, and a great idea in one location may work just as well in another.

Where some people find frustration in the lack of anti-trafficking efforts, others see opportunity. One of the most exciting aspects of the anti-trafficking movement is the field is wide open to new ideas and efforts. Many creative and passionate abolitionists have launched collaborative efforts in their hometown or on the other side of the world. Many have created new ways of fighting slavery. Find your passion, align it with your skills, and make something happen!

58 - How can businesses make a lasting impact on human trafficking?

Guest Contributor: Mark Wexler
Mark Wexler is a founder of Not For Sale, Just Business, Invention Hub, and co-creator of REBBL Tonic.

In February 2007 I launched Not For Sale, a global nonprofit, along with two friends, including Dr. David Batstone. We started the organization in response to a case of modern-day slavery in our own Northern California community.[3] Not For Sale has always possessed an intense entrepreneurial spirit as we worked toward ending slavery in our lifetime. As with many Bay Area startups, we have gone through iterations and pivots. However painful they were at the time, each turn has been essential to finding how we can have the greatest impact.

Our effort started as part of an awareness campaign around David's book *Not For Sale* and a Hollywood film about abolitionist William Wilberforce, *Amazing Grace*. For the first six months, we focused on raising donor funds for five partner anti-trafficking organizations via grassroots campaigning. With the urging of a major funder in the anti-slavery space, we shifted away from this model, and between late 2007 and 2011, we piloted a dozen direct service projects for survivors around the globe. As with any startup, some projects worked and have blossomed while others never made it out of the incubation stage.

In 2011 we hit our most important inflection point. We took a step back and came to the conclusion that, despite the hard work of many nonprofits, slavery would remain on a massive scale unless we invested in finding and launching new ways to fight it.

These stark facts served as our wakeup call:

- There are an estimated 21 million people in slavery today.[4]
- Slavery generates $150 billion annually for traffickers.[5]

- Slavery-fighting non-profits collectively raise somewhere around $150 million.

Bottom line: Modern-day slavery is a crime perpetrated by money-above-all-else business people. That's why we concluded that in addition to the political, policy, and enforcement efforts of others, the modern abolitionist movement required a business solution. We felt, based on our experiences and our Silicon Valley ties, uniquely positioned to engage immensely talented entrepreneurs and business leaders in that effort.

Today we are committing Not For Sale to organize and deploy talent and capital to fight modern-day slavery with capitalist fire.

We take a portfolio approach to fighting slavery, investing in a diverse set of partnerships and new businesses that have the potential to produce a multiplier effect—allowing us to have far greater impact than we ever could as a standalone non-profit.

Our social opportunity portfolio looks for compelling partners in areas where exploitation occurs and collaborates with them to assist survivors of modern-day slavery. This work builds on Not For Sale's record of supporting people after they had been trafficked. Overall since 2007 we've assisted nearly 10,500 survivors through in-depth support.[6] Not For Sale has had recent programming aimed at creating social opportunity for vulnerable people in Thailand, Amsterdam, Romania, Peru, and the San Francisco Bay Area. We have designs to add two new sites in the next six months with support from two corporate donor partners.

Our social enterprise portfolio addresses trafficking at its origin, assisting at-risk people. After identifying opportunities in at-risk communities, we will set out to inoculate those people from trafficking before it occurs. We will do this by creating long-term economic and community sustainability via the skills, jobs, and ongoing (healthy) connections to the marketplace offered by social enterprises.

This social enterprise portfolio is supported by our parent organization, Just Business, an incubator that identifies promising enterprises and connects them with investors, management teams, and other services they need to grow their businesses and impact. Just Business helps create incentives that focus entrepreneurs on the social and economic opportunity they can create.

Perhaps the best example of our social enterprise approach is REBBL, a beverage that was inspired to assist at-risk communities in the Peruvian Amazon. Today, nearly 130,000 pounds of certified fair trade and organic Brazil nuts are sold annually into the American and European marketplace by communities we set out to assist in 2010. Not For Sale helped secure the certifications and linked the communities to exporters. These were focused, strategic, philanthropic investments to help enhance the community's ability to leverage their herbal assets.

As a result of our success, we've been able to attract top business talent. Sheryl O'Loughlin, the former CEO of Clif Bar, is now REBBL's CEO. Rather than donating her time and talents, Sheryl has financial incentives to develop great products that make further community and environmental enhancement possible.

In 2014 more than 1.1 million products were sold in the U.S., European, Japanese, and Australian marketplaces that shed light on modern slavery, help amplify Not For Sale's story, and generate revenue for our social opportunity initiatives. These co-branded products highlight Not For Sale on their packaging, removing marketing costs from our economic bottom-line. In 2015 we're on trajectory to double the number of co-branded products sold—potentially surpassing 2.5 million products.

In return for our contributions to early-stage business development, Not For Sale's social enterprise portfolio produces 2.5% gross returns, founding equity, and a board seat to help maintain the social orientation of the social enterprises. The companies also have a supply chain transparency commitment built into their by-laws and when applicable, preferential treatment for employment opportunities for Not For Sale beneficiaries.

In 2016 we project that our social enterprise portfolio will cover over 50% of Not For Sale's overhead costs. Our goal in the future as our model strengthens is for the returns to be distributed via grant making to partners in our social opportunity portfolio.

Ultimately our hope is to build a replicable, self-sustaining business model that in time creates greater financial stability for the charitable direct-service projects Not For Sale supports. Simultaneously the model continues to create new connections with at-risk communities, helping generate more opportunities for social enterprise, education, training, and employment.

By fighting slavery, I've learned one clear lesson: It's not enough to work hard within a system that perpetuates the problem you want to solve. To find a solution, we must also step outside our old, traditional structures and create new models of social change—including building new justice-focused businesses.

Together we can, and will, create a world in which no one is for sale.

59 - How can FBOs help?

Guest Contributor: Sandra Morgan
Sandra Morgan, PhD, RN, directs the Global Center for Women and Justice at Vanguard University of Southern California and cohosts the Ending Human Trafficking podcast. A past administrator of the Orange County Human Trafficking Task Force, Sandra has presented training in Argentina, Bulgaria, Greece, Italy, Iraq, Romania, and Russia, and at the United Nations.

Faith Based Organizations (FBOs), whether churches, mosques, synagogues, temples, or other religious communities, have a natural platform from which to contribute to many aspects of combatting human trafficking and slavery. These groups are organized around common values with established infrastructure. They are already engaged in serving their communities and especially, serving those in need.

The passage of the Trafficking Victims Protection Act in 2000 generated new awareness of human trafficking and the need for community education; as a result, many faith-based leaders rallied their congregations to respond to the crisis. However, as this movement grows, it is imperative that efforts are sustainable and follow best practice models that ensure the safety and well-being of the volunteers as well as the victims.

Best practices for community engagement in anti-trafficking are built on the 4P model as described by the Global Trafficking in Persons report authorized by the Trafficking Victims Protection Act (TVPA). The four Ps are Prevention, Protection, Prosecution and Partnership. This model identifies professional and community roles that are necessary for a sustainable response to human trafficking. Organizations may have members who are professionals within law enforcement and victim services, or who volunteer to serve in areas where professional credentials are legal requirements, such as health and dental care.

As members of the community, Faith Based Organizations are committed to collaboration that will support the TVPA and that fall within the definition of the fourth P: Partnership. Partnership was described in the 2010 Trafficking in Persons Report as being based on identifying the unique expertise and resources available for the local effort across the first 3Ps of Prevention, Protection, and Prosecution. A careful assessment of expertise and resources will result in a sustainable and consistent compassionate response that respects the intersection of public and private roles as these individuals work together in local communities.

Each faith community or congregation is unique, so there are no "one size fits all" strategies. However, successful partnership begins with these three steps:

1. Identify the expertise and resources inside your faith community.
2. Study the issue and learn the professional language of the human trafficking community.
3. Assess local need.

The first step to prepare to join the battle is to do an assessment of available expertise and resources. This evaluation should include existing ministries, member skills, and community activities. Plans to fight human trafficking often begin with "Let's start … (fill in the blank)." But often these groups may already be doing something that is a critical prevention strategy, such as an afterschool program in a high-risk neighborhood. In addition, members may have years of children's education experience, and facilities may include classrooms furnished by age group.

The second step is to learn more about human trafficking, especially the root causes that increase vulnerability for youth and adults to be exploited for labor or for commercial sex. Local expertise and resources can bridge the critical gap in prevention. In addition, it is especially important to learn the professional language for two reasons. First, it will help FBO volunteers interface with law enforcement and victim services in a professional manner. Second, it will reduce the risk of using language that misrepresents the crime and dehumanizes victims. It is important to understand that the language used by media is designed to sell the news, the story, or the film and may often sensationalize at the cost of personal dignity.

The third step is to assess the local need. As a practitioner I have often wondered at the passion and resources a local congregation invests *over there*, without demonstrating awareness of the need in their own backyard. A community assessment will uncover risk for modern slavery in labor markets as well as commercial sexual exploitation. I recommend that groups begin with a simple exercise: I draw a tree and ask the group to identify problems in their community. Individuals add specific problems to the leaves. Then we begin to draw the roots and identify why those problems exist. For instance, one community identified homeless youth as a leaf on their tree. They knew that homeless youth are more vulnerable to recruitment by traffickers. They had done outreach to homeless youth passing out cards with the hotline number and warning them about taking jobs promising unrealistic wages. But now they looked at the roots and asked, "Why are there so many homeless youth?" They did some research and discovered that the local school district had a homeless youth liaison who had a need for volunteers. It was not as exciting as going out on a rescue at 1:00 A.M., but it became a very rewarding community partnership that was sustainable and made a difference.

Consider, for example, the experience of a small urban church that assessed their expertise and resources in relationship to the need in their community. Their facility was located only a block away from a middle school. The church had classrooms (a resource) that were only being used twice a week. Two of their members were experienced teachers (an expertise). They did not have significant financial resources, but they learned about the excellent Netsmartz cyber-safety prevention resources that had already been developed and funded in part by U.S. tax dollars. (The Internet Safety curriculum is available at http://www.

netsmartz.org/Parents). This local church may not have had expertise in Internet safety, but they had a resource—a children's classroom—and other expertise—teaching experience—which they combined to offer their community an excellent prevention tool while telling their neighbors, "We care about your children."

It is important for faith-based communities to consider these three steps as they join the battle to end modern day slavery. There are many benefits that reduce duplication of efforts and thereby steward resources well. But there are also risks when groups plunge in without careful evaluation. Community reputation can be damaged when commitments are made and then not sustained. But even more important are the risks associated with the victims who may be unintentionally placed in harm's way or re-victimized by efforts to raise awareness or raise funds.

There are many local, state, and federal programs that need volunteers and partners in order to continue to serve victims of human trafficking. Professionals within FBOs often volunteer to provide pro bono services to victims, including dental and medical care, counseling, life skills mentoring, and even haircuts! These are examples of the fourth P, Partnership—that builds a community safety net using our expertise and resources.

I also encourage those in the faith-based community to use their established values and infrastructure to fill the Prevention gap. Existing education programs for children and adults can include prevention strategies that protect children and conduct outreach programs that implement demand reduction strategies, tactics which address the media's normalization of hyper-sexualization and offer recovery programs for pornography addiction.

Becoming a partner in the battle against human trafficking will enhance a faith-based organization's community presence when it is done with the community. This standard requires that they play by the rules, do not take shortcuts—and promote excellence in everything. Protecting the dignity and privacy of victims should be the fundamental standard for FBO efforts as it is across the spectrum for those working to end human trafficking.

60 - What signs of trafficking can we learn to recognize?

This question cannot be addressed without considering the perspective of the observer and context of the observation. *Perspective* speaks to our awareness that trafficking exists and that trafficking can be recognized in the course of professional activities or other observations. *Context* refers to being aware of how signs of trafficking can vary according to the circumstances in which they are observed. The signs of trafficking a police officer observes might be different from those recognized by a victim advocate or an emergency room nurse.

Of the two, perspective is most important. If I can help someone become aware that trafficking exists and instill in them a feeling of responsibility to be aware of signs, they will quickly understand the signs within the context of their role or in the environment where their observations may take place.

When I train law enforcement investigators, the first part of the training focuses on defining modern slavery, illustrating how victims are exploited, and explaining why the topic should be important to them and their community. Often it can be challenging to change their perspective, especially regarding the sex trade, as some in law enforcement believe it should be easy for victims to walk away from those who victimize them. To shift this perspective, I often use the analogy of domestic violence victims who are abused over a long period of time before they gain the strength to leave or who return again and again to their abuser.

But once a professional's perspective changes, it becomes easier for them to view trafficking within the context of their work; the signs begin to appear obvious. The police officer may recognize that the quiet and fearful-looking person who is described as a "relative" may be a forced domestic servant or that the "child prostitute" is a victim of commercial sexual exploitation. In the same manner, an emergency room nurse or doctor treating a person for illness or injury may wonder why the patient doesn't speak for himself or why the patient's "friend" does most of the talking. They may recognize the possibly that the "friend" is actually a trafficker there to prevent the victim from disclosing the facts of the situation.

Trafficking is too complex to be approached with a simple list of signs to be looked for (though we will try, later). But once we possess the perspective that trafficking is limited only by the imagination and coercive power of the trafficker and that it can be found anywhere, we can begin to recognize the significance of subtle signs of control, isolation, or unreasonable fear—particularly in victims unwilling to talk about their situation.

Today, slavery exists outside the perspective and context of slavery most of us carry in our mind. The modern abolitionist changes their perspective and their understanding of context in order to see slavery and exploitation where most people miss it.

61 - Which professions should receive training on human trafficking?

Several key professional sectors must receive training on human trafficking and the multisector response: street-level law enforcement and detectives, prosecutors, and the broad range of professionals within the victim-services sector, such as case managers, advocates, attorneys, and shelter staff.

But what other specific professions are *worth the investment of time and effort* to train? Training and outreach involve time, energy, and cost, so these efforts should be examined in terms of return on investment. Not every profession offers the same potential return, due to several factors.

Certain professionals can be classified as *high-potential identifiers* of trafficking victims. For example, Emergency Room nurses and doctors see dozens of patients every day, potentially including trafficking victims. But a less valuable audience might be nurses who work in an Intensive Care Unit, as they see fewer patients per day. This does not mean ICU nurses should not be trained, only that the potential impact of any training they receive may not have a result equivalent to that of nurses who see more patients from a broad cross-section of the population.

Social workers, judges, and juvenile hall and probation staff members are all good candidates for training not only because they may recognize signs of victimization in their clients but also because they play key roles in the broader system through which struggling or marginalized persons pass. And traffickers seek marginalized people to victimize.

There is a difference between raising awareness and training. The first informs, the second provides instruction on what to do with that information. Both can be valuable to anyone, but the return on the effort can vary greatly.

Professionals who are mandated reporters are familiar and comfortable with the reporting process and therefore more likely to report a suspected human trafficking incident. The staff in a hospital emergency room, for example, is already familiar with the signs of sexual assault, domestic violence, and child abuse. In most cases, they are mandated by law to report suspected cases. In addition, their professional ethic as caregivers increases the likelihood they will act to aid a victim. In this case, training mostly consists of changing the perspective of nurses and doctors so they understand slavery exists and victims of trafficking may come into their emergency room for aid. They already know whom to call, how to report suspected incidents, and where to refer victims needing assistance. Similarly, schoolteachers are trained to recognize signs of abuse and to report their suspicions. In most circumstances, they too are mandated reporters. (These laws vary by state, and being a mandated reporter can depend upon the crime. For example, suspected child abuse must be reported, but the laws of most states don't mandate the reporting of suspected trafficking.)

Some suggest training cable TV installers or other public utility professionals who, due to their work around a great number of homes and businesses, might see signs of trafficking. But these professionals are not mandated reporters, and looking for victims of trafficking is in no way directly related to their work. This is not to demean any sector of professionals; every group can contribute in the fight against human trafficking. But the effort required to gain access to these types of professionals and conduct training will not have the same return as training other professionals. It just makes sense to weigh these factors when deciding where to invest training efforts and resources.

Unique circumstances can also create training opportunities. For instance, many communities seek to provide training on human trafficking to their local hospitality industry (hotel, motel, and restaurant) staff in advance of the Super Bowl or other large-scale events. These events open the door to training opportunities because the event provides the context in which victims might be observed. In this case, changing the perspective of those receiving the training may have a positive impact.

Raising awareness of trafficking, of how traffickers operate, and of the resources available locally to assist victims is vital.

Creating, scheduling, and presenting awareness and training programs requires a major investment. Work to impact the professional sectors in your community where the most potential benefit can be found.

Often, the best training results come from hiring consultants experienced in anti-trafficking work who can train the community's law enforcement and service providers. It makes little sense to train other potential identifiers if those who will help a victim or investigate the case have not been trained themselves.

62 - What questions can help identify a victim?

Identifying trafficking victims or incidents cannot be reduced to a simple checklist of signs or answers to a series of questions. Much depends upon the perspective of the observer and context of the situation. But let's examine a few potential questions which could be asked of a suspected victim and then, more importantly, what to do next.

The intent of these questions is not to definitively identify a trafficking victim. Rather it is intended to help the person having contact with a suspected victim assess their suspicions before reporting to the proper agency. These questions should be used as a screening tool only. Only law enforcement officers, victim advocates, or attorneys should interview the suspected victim in detail.

Reasonable questions to ask include:

- Has anyone hurt you, or threatened to hurt you or your family?
- Are you free to leave your job or the person you work for?
- Does your employer hold your earnings from you?
- Do you owe part of your earnings to your employer?
- What would happen if you tried to leave your job? (or boyfriend, if sex trafficking is suspected)
- Can you freely communicate with your family or friends when you want to?
- Have you been told the police will arrest you if you go to them for help?
- Do you feel isolated from family, friends, or community?
- Are you forced to engage in sex for money?
- Does someone else hold your passport or identification documents?

None of these ten questions specifically asks, "Are you a victim of human trafficking?" because we know most victims do not self-identify with that term. These are general questions, but the answers given could suggest whether the individual is a potential trafficking victim.

Again, these questions should be used as a screening tool only; if the answer to one or more of these questions leads you to believe the person may be a victim, stop and phone the local police and/or a local human trafficking organization with the capability and expertise to respond. If in doubt, phone the National Human Trafficking Hotline (888-373-7888), and they will attempt to coordinate a response.

Do not delve more deeply into the victim's story unless they share it with you without prompting. In this case, let them talk and be prepared to report what you hear to the police investigator. Do not ask questions about the incident; you may inadvertently create problems related to confidentiality for the victim (and yourself) in the future.

The National Human Trafficking Resource Center website offers additional helpful information under the title, *Human Trafficking: Recognize the Signs.*[7]

With only a short list of questions and the willingness and knowledge to report suspicions, anyone can help identify a victim of human trafficking.

63 - What types of anti-trafficking jobs exist?

Openings are limited, but more jobs in this field become available every year. In the past, job openings were filled primarily through word-of-mouth. Today, job openings are posted online, have increased in number, and include specific guidelines for preferred skills and experience.

For those interested in law enforcement, there are two potential routes to becoming a human trafficking investigator. Regardless of the route selected, the process is long and does not guarantee a job investigating human trafficking.

The first option is federal law enforcement, primarily with the Federal Bureau of Investigation, though the Department of Labor and the Department of Homeland Security Immigration and Customs Enforcement also have roles in investigating human trafficking. This path follows a lengthy process of applying, testing, being selected for a background investigation, receiving a job offer, completing academy training, getting assigned to a field office where human trafficking is investigated, and finally, being assigned to investigate cases. Though daunting, it can be done. I once had a colleague who, while working as a nurse, decided she wanted to investigate human trafficking as an FBI agent. She completed every step outlined above. When we met, she was investigating human trafficking cases in Northern California.

Local law enforcement is also an option. Becoming a detective for a local agency follows a similar path. After successfully completing the application and selection process, the candidate must complete police academy training and then work patrol or other field assignments before becoming a detective. The likelihood of investigating human trafficking then depends upon the size of the city and agency. Not every local agency is involved with a task force. But again, it is possible to achieve this goal with perseverance—and an opportunity within the right agency.

Attorneys have more options, such as pursuing a position as a prosecutor with the United States Attorney's Office or a county or state prosecutor's office. Attorneys can also become involved assisting victims with immigration issues or civil actions.

Working with a VSP or NGO is another avenue into the field. Positions include providing direct services to clients, potentially including victims of human trafficking. These positions include case managers and victim advocates. Some of these jobs are entry-level positions requiring minimal formal education while others may require a B.A. or M.A. degree in Social Work or a related field.

Yet another avenue of employment can be found doing outreach or advocacy work for an NGO, FBO, or MANGO. This option may not include direct contact with victims, but opportunities exist for those with a gift for educating others on human trafficking.

Job opportunities may be located in the United States or abroad, and the education and experience required can vary greatly. (I post all job opportunities I learn of on The Essential Abolitionist Facebook page.)

If these avenues don't excite for you, consider this option: Create the job yourself. The response to slavery is wide open, and many people have created their own niche (and career) by aligning their skills and experience with their passion to be an abolitionist. Think about what you would like to do, then start inquiring with trafficking experts to determine whether your idea has promise. Most abolitionists are happy to share their passion and opinions with others wishing to get involved. Artists, writers, photographers, those with information technology skills, all these and more have found a way to turn their passion into a career.

The fight against slavery can be fought in many ways. Start dreaming about how you can make a difference today.

64 - Why is self-care important for abolitionists?

Self-care refers to each of us taking care of ourselves. Every job entails some form of stress, whether physical, emotional, or both.

Victim advocates, police investigators, and others who work closely with victims of crime face issues related to their work, including burnout and symptoms of PTSD. It is sad to see those who devote their energies (and sometimes their entire lives) to helping others become depressed, cynical, and unhappy. It is even worse to see work-related stress lead to failed relationships or substance abuse.

Anyone interested in an anti-trafficking career should keep this in mind, recognize the risks, and take care to avoid damaging their own lives or those close to them. A few simple steps can help reduce many of the potential problems related to work-related stress.

First, go home at the end of the day. Be able to leave the job behind and enjoy your family and friends. While this can be difficult after a long and stressful day, making your family and friends a priority is vital. Also, maintain friendships with people outside your profession and place of work.

Get some exercise; have some fun; engage in a hobby (or two) that doesn't have a connection to work.

It can be sad, at times, to assist victims of crime. But it is even sadder to see someone who was once bright-eyed, energetic, and passionate, lose these traits in the course of helping others. Taking care of ourselves gives us the strength, support, optimism, and passion to help others for many years to come.

CHAPTER 7

Human Trafficking: Myths & Misconceptions

*There are a thousand hacking at the branches of evil
to one who is striking at the root.*
THOREAU

In a complex and dynamic environment like the response to human trafficking, misunderstandings occur. Efforts to simplify complex topics and issues to make them fit within the confines of media can quickly contribute to the likelihood that myths and misconceptions will arise—especially in the realm of social media where memes replace analysis or space for explanation is limited. The high level of passion among abolitionists can also increase the likelihood that incorrect information can take on a life of its own. Myths and misconceptions are a part of modern slavery; here are some of the most common.

65 - Is the Super Bowl the "largest human trafficking incident" in the United States?

In the run-up to the 2011 Super Bowl in Arlington, Texas, the Texas Attorney General (now Governor) Greg Abbott made several comments regarding human trafficking and the Super Bowl including, "It's commonly known as the single largest human trafficking incident in the United States."[1]

Like any good myth, this comment went viral and took on a life of its own. It is now common in the weeks before the Super

Bowl to see news articles and social media posts promoting this myth. Yet little evidence exists supporting this claim.

The Arizona State University School of Social Work closely examined human trafficking surrounding both the 2014 Super Bowl in New Jersey and the 2015 Super Bowl in Arizona.[2] Though the results were inconclusive, this study includes a useful examination of online advertising, levels of demand, and other topics related to online advertising of commercial sex. The report, issued in February 2015, states,

> *In years past, media reports have speculated that the Super Bowl was one of the most prominent national events where sex trafficking occurs; however, researchers have yet to substantiate these statements. While there is no empirical evidence that the Super Bowl causes an increase in sex trafficking compared to other days and events throughout the year, there was a noticeable increase in those activities intended to locate victims from both law enforcement and service provision organizations.*

The statement includes a significant observation: the increase in law enforcement and VSP activities *aimed at locating victims*. Any increase in effort to locate victims and traffickers *should increase results*. This—by itself—should not be seen as proof of an increase in human trafficking around the Super Bowl.

In recent years temporary task forces have been created within the host city to focus on human trafficking, typically operating from the weekend before the game through Super Bowl Sunday, about ten days. The most basic research methodology would demand a control study with the same effort being made, for the same amount of time, in the same or a similar city. The Arizona State University study points to this lack of control groups and other research challenges that need to be addressed.

Exacerbating this myth are headlines like this from a 2015 *Los Angeles Times* article, "National sex trafficking sting nets nearly 600 arrests before Super Bowl."[3] The casual reader may believe the article cites arrests in the host city, but the article actually addresses sting operations in 17 states during the two weeks before the Super Bowl.

The Super Bowl, like any other major event in a large city, provides an opportunity for crime to increase, including sex trafficking. Dispelling this myth is not to say trafficking doesn't occur at all at the Super Bowl, but focusing on specific events can give the impression that anti-trafficking activities are important only at specific times. But we know the truth: Sex and labor trafficking occur every day, and efforts need to be consistent every day of the year.

66 - Do Hollywood movies accurately portray human trafficking?

No—or at least not yet.

The 2008 film Taken, starring Liam Neeson, is a hugely popular movie with a plot involving human trafficking. When traffickers kidnap his daughter (in truth, kidnapping is a rare occurrence relative to the number of victims of trafficking), Neeson's character, a retired CIA agent with "special skills," goes on the hunt for the kidnappers. There is a lot of violent retribution. It is an action film first, foremost, and last. But for many, this film provides their only base of knowledge regarding human trafficking.

Most Hollywood films depicting human trafficking focus on sex trafficking. Many TV dramas have included episodes featuring human trafficking in the plot line, and reality TV has made its attempts to simplify the complexity of human trafficking. But movies and television shows are produced to make money, not necessarily to accurately portray a complex topic like human trafficking. When watching these films, cast a critical eye on how accurately the movie depicts trafficking and the methods for liberating victims.

Movie viewings are popular public awareness tools and can be a catalyst for generating informative discussions. My favorite movie for introducing others to human trafficking is The Dark Side of Chocolate,[4] a 2010 documentary examining the use of child labor for harvesting cocoa in West Africa. I like this film because it illustrates the complexity of the cocoa trade, how easily children can be exploited when there are few options for work or education, and how difficult it is for international agencies to respond. The movie focuses on labor trafficking, a rarity in the human trafficking genre. Most importantly, the movie touches every one of us because we all enjoy chocolate! The movie informs us that as consumers, each of us can be the unwitting beneficiary of forced labor.

It's hard to make an exciting, action-packed movie about domestic servitude or working in a sweat shop with actors portraying victim advocates, immigration attorneys, and police officers—who all spend hours interviewing victims to unearth their story of victimization. But that is the reality of the response to human trafficking.

67 - Does comparing the African slave trade with modern slavery make sense?

"There are more slaves today than during the entire African Slave trade." This popular social media meme is used to draw attention to human trafficking. It is catchy, and it is true. But the statement lacks context. The knowledgeable abolitionist should be aware of a few additional facts.

The African slave trade is generally considered to span from the 1500s to the 1800s, roughly a 400-year period, when an estimated 11 million Africans were forcibly taken from their home and transported to Europe and the Americas. It was an epic violation of human rights.

The world's population in 1800 is estimated to have been one billion people. Today, estimates place the planet's population at seven billion people, a seven-fold increase since 1800. The International Labour Organization's estimate of 21 million people enslaved today is nearly double the number of all slaves removed from Africa over nearly 400 years. (Just as we don't know exactly how many people are enslaved today, researchers don't know exactly how many victims were removed from Africa, and this number does not include their descendants who were also enslaved.)

For the abolitionist helping others understand human trafficking, this historical background might be interesting, but the complicated context for comparing the two should also be established.

68 - If victims are not locked and chained, why do we see these images?

Good question. Why *are* these images used?

The concepts of slavery, forced labor, or forced sexual exploitation are communicated through images of locks, chains, barbed wire, or wrists bound by rope because most viewers will immediately associate these images with violence, slavery, or a lack of freedom. These images catch our eye and our imaginations. While some incidents of trafficking do involve physical constraint, these images don't reflect the more common reality of modern slavery; most victims are not held by chains—but by force, fraud, or coercion.

Creating visual messages about human trafficking that convey the more abstract reality of threats and coercion is a huge challenge. Until creative abolitionists come up with ways to depict human trafficking without these images, we will continue to see them.

69 - What are the connections between prostitution, pornography, and trafficking?

Guest Contributor: Melissa Farley
Melissa Farley is a psychologist and Executive Director of Prostitution Research & Education. Melissa has 49 publications in the field of violence against women, most of which address prostitution, pornography, and sex trafficking.

Pornography is an act of prostitution. A survivor of prostitution explained, "Pornography is prostitution that is legalized as long as someone gets to take pictures." Pornography documents and facilitates trafficking.

The argument that prostitution is a job is made from the perspective of pimps and sex buyers, not from the perspective of those in it. For those in it, prostitution is not a job, it is "paid-for rape."

Please don't mystify the sex industry. Don't assume it's vastly different from other types of exploitation and human cruelty. The real lives of those who are trafficked or prostituted or made into pornography are often indistinguishable from the real lives of victims of rape, incest, and intimate partner violence. The main difference is money. Profits turn sexual assault of children, rape, domestic violence, humiliation, and sexual harassment—and pictures taken of those things—into a business enterprise.

The emotional consequences of prostitution and trafficking are the same in widely varying cultures whether it's pornography or trafficking, high class or low class, legal or illegal—whether in a brothel, strip club, massage parlor, or the street. Symptoms of emotional distress among those in the sex trade are off the charts: depression, suicidality, post-traumatic stress disorder, dissociation, substance abuse. Two-thirds of women, men, and transgenders in prostitution in nine countries met diagnostic criteria for post-traumatic stress disorder. This level of emotional distress is the same as the most emotionally traumatized people studied by psychologists—battered women, raped women, combat vets, and torture survivors.

In the real world, from the perspective of the person in the sex trade—pornography, prostitution, and sex trafficking are the same. More than 80% of the time, adult women in the sex industry are under pimp control—that is what trafficking is.[5] Pornography meets the legal definition of trafficking if the pornographer recruits, entices, or obtains women for the purpose of photographing live commercial sex acts.

Like other global businesses, the sex industry has domestic and international sectors, marketing sectors, and a range of physical locations out of which sex businesses operate. There are many different owners and managers, and the business of sexual exploitation is constantly expanding as technology, law, and public opinion permit.

Pornographers are specialty pimps who use pornography to advertise prostitution and to traffic women. For example, Backpage.com, owned by a Dutch company, advertises and sells pornography and facilitates trafficking in the U.S. As a Massachusetts Attorney General said, "Most of the human trafficking cases that our office has prosecuted involve advertisements on Backpage."

Here is an example of the links between pornography, prostitution, and trafficking: Glenn Marcus ran a torture pornography website. He psychologically coerced a woman to permit pornography of her to be sold on Slavespace.com. At one point he stuffed a ball gag in her mouth, sewed her mouth shut, and hung her on a wall. She brought charges against Marcus who was her pimp/pornographer/trafficker—and torturer. Her attorneys used the following definition: *Sex trafficking is coercing or selling a person into a situation of sexual exploitation, such as prostitution or pornography.* On March 5, 2007, pornographer Marcus was convicted of sex trafficking. This legal decision reflects a deepening understanding of the ways in which pornography, prostitution, and trafficking are the same for the person who is being sexually coerced and exploited for profit.

Another example of these links: The convergence of different arms of the sex industry can be seen in a law enforcement action in Las Vegas. A sex business—that looked like an office complex from the street—blended pornography production and trafficking with escort and webcam prostitution. (On a webcam site, the sex buyer pays to chat with women who prostitute on streaming video, performing in real time what masturbating sex buyers pay them to do.) In this case, the pimp/pornographer rented six offices that functioned as Internet pornography businesses, and as cyber-prostitution via webcam, and a place where women were pimped out to hotels and to a brothel. Nevada has legal pimping in rurally zoned brothels, but prostitution in Las Vegas is illegal, so when the women were pimped out to Las Vegas hotels, that is trafficking.

The same oppressive experiences channel women into pornography, prostitution, and trafficking. Childhood abuse and neglect, a lack of quality education and job training opportunities, culturally mainstreamed misogyny, along with racism and poverty—all coerce women into the sex trade. Women are coerced into pornography by deception, threats, or violence. A survivor of pornography and prostitution explained that she had been pressured to do more extreme sex acts on film, was physically hurt, and was raped on film—just the way women in prostitution are pressured by pimps and sex buyers to perform more harmful and dangerous sex acts.

The same kinds of violence against women are perpetrated in pornography, prostitution, and trafficking. Women in prostitution face a likelihood of weekly rape. A Canadian woman in prostitution said, "*What is rape for others, is normal for us.*" A woman at a Nevada legal brothel explained that legal prostitution was "*like you sign a contract to be raped.*" Research showed that sex buyers had the same risk factors as men who commit sexual aggression: a preference for impersonal sex, fear of rejection by women, past history of rape, willingness to rape, attitudes of sexual entitlement, low empathy, and a perception of women in prostitution/pornography as intrinsically different from other women.[6]

Why do sex industry advocates de-link pornography, prostitution and trafficking?

The answer is because it increases profits. Disconnecting trafficking from prostitution and pornography normalizes most of the sex industry. Here's how the de-linking works: Every time an adjective is put in front of the word prostitution, pornography, or trafficking, it falsely carves out a group of human beings who we allow to be sold for sex. For example, forced vs. voluntary trafficking—it's assumed that some people volunteer to traffic themselves; child vs. adult pornography—it's assumed to be normal and mainstreamed to make pornography of adults; illegal vs. legal prostitution—it's assumed that legal prostitution reduces harm and thus is acceptable.

Did we de-link child from adult slavery? Did abolitionists focus on saving child slaves, leaving their parents behind? No we did not. Do we de-link severe from not-so-severe domestic violence? Do advocates focus on only the most extreme cases and leave behind the woman who "only" has bruises but no broken bones? No we do not. Abolitionists seek to shut down the sex industry—all of it.

70 - Are all sex workers victims of human trafficking?

I was part of a panel discussion on human trafficking, addressing an audience of law enforcement executives, when one of the attendees posed this question to another panelist, a local prosecutor. The prosecutor's reply was "Yes. All sex workers are victims of trafficking."

But this answer isn't correct. For a person involved in commercial sex to be a victim of human trafficking, there must be the element of force, fraud, or coercion, or they must be under age 18. This prosecutor (and many other individuals) believes that no one would willingly engage in commercial sex without some type of compelling force or coercion. But there are sex workers (this is the term they prefer) who willingly engage in commercial sex. Many become advocates for other sex workers, and it is not uncommon to see sex worker organizations oppose anti-trafficking laws they perceive as being detrimental to their profession. This begs the question, how many sex workers engage in commercial sex freely, and how many are under some element of force, fraud, or coercion?

Melissa Farley, Ph.D., who addressed the links between pornography, prostitution, and trafficking in the previous question, has explored this subject extensively. Based upon an examination of eighteen different estimates from research studies, government reports, and NGOs, Melissa believes at least 84% of women in prostitution are under third-party control (pimped or trafficked).[7] (This particular estimate focuses on women only.) Melissa believes this a conservative estimate, and some researchers believe the percentage is higher.

While it can be difficult to distinguish prostitution activity from commercial sex exploitation, it is clear the number of truly voluntary sex workers is a small percentage. For the majority of those involved in commercial sex someone else is controlling—to some extent—the actions of the person engaging in the sex. This person is not a sex worker; they are an exploited person.

Regardless of the exact number, only a small percentage of those engaged in commercial sex engage in this work by choice, and few are free to quit whenever they choose.

Also, while life circumstances may "force" a person into the sex trade, individuals cannot exploit themselves; another person must apply the force, fraud, or coercion for trafficking to occur.

We should be aware of these distinctions when discussing the sex trade and human trafficking. Moral views aside, the criminal elements of human trafficking and commercial sexual exploitation are clear.

71 - Are low-cost services based on labor trafficking?

Low-cost services can, of course, be based on labor trafficking. But paying a lower than expected cost for a service does not guarantee trafficking victims were exploited in performing the work.

This particular question often arises in relation to nail salons. While trafficking victims have been identified working in nail salons, this question offers us another opportunity to examine human trafficking within the context of a business model and our preconceived ideas about possible victims.

I know of a nail salon in an up-scale shopping complex in the San Francisco Bay Area that offers excellent service at a price that many clients perceive as too inexpensive to be legitimate. The women working in this salon are primarily from Southeast Asia and often have limited English-speaking skills. The workers sometimes avoid looking their clients directly in the eye. Clients who are aware of how and where trafficking can occur sometimes question whether these women could be trafficking victims. After all, if the price of a manicure or pedicure is so low, it must be based upon slave labor, right? I know clients have this perception because I've been asked this question—about the same salon—many times.

When our task force looked into the situation, we found the employees were being paid minimum wage plus tips. The employees were guaranteed only four hours of work; after that, they would be sent home unless there were other clients to be served. By tightly controlling the cost of labor (typically the largest expense of any business), the salon owner was able to offer the salon services for a lower-than-expected fee.

Other factors in this scenario influenced suspicions: the workers' nationality, their limited ability to speak English, and their lack of eye contact. But the San Francisco Bay Area contains one of the largest Southeast Asian populations in the United States, so being from Southeast Asia is not out of the ordinary.

Many immigrants have limited English skills, and within some cultures, looking directly into another person's eyes can be seen as impolite or challenging another's authority. While these factors *could be potential indicators* of trafficking, considering these factors in the context of this particular salon is essential to interpreting this case.

Circumstances like those described above can lead to discussions of other important topics related to human trafficking—in this case, the discussion of "living" wages. Low-wage jobs exist, with and without human trafficking.

Though the labor in this particular nail salon was not forced, this scenario illustrates the power of knowledge of human trafficking among the general population; these same observations and actions (i.e., contacting law enforcement to investigate) could have led to the discovery of a trafficking incident. I applaud the perceptive skills of the women who asked me about this salon!

A critical point to remember is this: If employees feel free to leave their job, they probably are not victims of human trafficking.

72 - Should every case of trafficking be prosecuted as trafficking?

This question frequently arises when a high-profile criminal case catches the public's interest and includes, or appears to include, human trafficking. Some question why suspects are not charged with trafficking in these circumstances.

But one simple reason dominates the rationale: The defendant's other crimes are so egregious that "stacking on" the charge of human trafficking will have little or no impact on the final sentencing. For instance, if a suspect has kidnapped someone, sexually assaulted them, and then forced them into commercial sexual exploitation, the kidnapping and sexual assault statutes alone may put the offender in prison for life. In this case, a prosecutor has little to gain from charging the suspect with human trafficking. In fact, should this case go to trial, the prosecutor now has to explain human trafficking to the jury in addition to explaining the other crimes. While most jurors understand kidnapping and sexual assault, they may not be familiar with human trafficking.

Also, as already mentioned, there is the possibility the law enforcement agency and prosecutor handling the case have not received training on identifying and prosecuting trafficking cases.

These are just two reasons why charging an offender with human trafficking may not occur, though the case may appear to include modern slavery.

73 - Do high prison sentences reduce human trafficking?

The impulse to imprison traffickers is understandable. Traffickers who exploit the vulnerable—particularly the youngest victims—should be imprisoned for a very long time indeed. That is my opinion, and one shared by most people.

In theory, prison sentencing helps prevent crime in two ways. First, incarceration removes the opportunity for the offender to commit crime; a person in prison can't commit crime. The second is achieved through deterrence. A potential offender may decide not to engage in a particular criminal activity for fear of going to prison. In theory, the higher the potential sentence, the higher the level of deterrence.

But there is very little empirical evidence supporting the contention that higher prison sentences *prevent* crime, and in 25 years of police work, I never met a criminal who examined the penal code to check the potential prison sentences before committing a crime.

Raising prison sentences alone will have limited—if any—impact on human trafficking. To be clear, I'm not opposed to high prison sentences. As a police officer investigating sex crimes, I was always trying to get the highest sentence possible depending upon the background of the offender and the circumstances of the crime. But high prison sentencing standards alone should not be promoted as an effective way of preventing crime.

The most effective means of using criminal sentencing to impact human trafficking is to *prosecute and imprison for human trafficking*. As examined previously, the biggest challenge in law enforcement is training those on the front lines to effectively investigate, prosecute, and obtain convictions for human trafficking charges. Before campaigning for higher prison sentences, we should examine how often current human trafficking statutes are being used and increase the awareness and expertise of police and prosecutors. These actions will increase human trafficking convictions.

Prison sentences also carry the high costs associated with incarceration. As a result, legislators may resist increasing prison sentences simply based on expense. This obstacle presents another reason abolitionists might be more effective by focusing on how current laws are employed—rather than on raising prison sentences.

I offer an additional thought, purely my own opinion, based upon my experience assisting victims of many different types of crime. Some people seek higher sentencing standards for sex trafficking than labor trafficking, usually viewing commercial sex exploitation as a form of sexual assault and therefore more heinous than labor exploitation. But consider these situations: An 8-year-old girl is forced to work as a domestic servant, beaten and abused until she is freed *four years later*; or the woman enslaved as a domestic servant for *eighteen years*—over half her life—before being identified. Should their victimizations be deemed less heinous because they were not forced into commercial sex? I'll leave this question open for discussion.

Alas, there are no quick fixes to modern slavery. The complexities should now be apparent. There is a popular anti-trafficking slogan used to point out the difficulty of identifying trafficking victims within the hidden world of modern slavery: "Look beneath the surface." When examining our collective approach to modern slavery, we also need to look beneath the surface for what can be truly effective.

74 - Is a "john" also a trafficker?

Is a buyer of sex the same as a sex trafficker? The answer to this question is tricky and depends upon one's perspective. Many believe there is no difference between a john and a trafficker and that a buyer of sex should be criminally charged with trafficking. But what really matters is what the law says.

The TVPA (2000) definition of commercial sex trafficking, "in which a commercial sex act is induced by force, fraud, or coercion, or in which the person induced to perform such act has not yet attained 18 years of age,"[8] *speaks to the person inducing the force, fraud, or coercion,* not the person purchasing the sex act. To date, most state laws reflect this language.

However, the Justice for Victims of Trafficking Act of 2015 changed federal law to include whoever "patronizes, or solicits by any means a person" (in other words, pays for engaging in commercial sex), "knowing, or [...] in reckless disregard of the fact, that means of force, threats of force, fraud, coercion [...] will be used to cause the person to engage in a commercial sex act, or that the person has not attained the age of 18 years" (18 U.S. Code § 1591).[9]

So now, under federal law, prosecutors have the discretion to charge a buyer of sex under the statute originally applicable only to traffickers—if the legal specifications above are met.

The change in the statute has its detractors, with some abolitionists believing the serious charge of trafficking should be used only for those who are exploiting others using force, fraud, or coercion and profiting from that exploitation.

Those who favor prosecuting buyers as traffickers see the new law as a powerful tool to reduce the demand for commercial sex; if it becomes known that johns now face much higher penal risks, demand may drop.

State laws vary, and ultimately, the decision of which charges to bring against any offender lies with the prosecutor.

The prosecution of johns alongside sex traffickers is but one point on which many abolitionists argue. Disagreement on elements of criminal law, response philosophies and practices, and other topics are a very real part of the anti-trafficking movement. The response to trafficking is dynamic. While this constant motion can be frustrating at times, it fosters new ideas. Debates arise from passion, and opposition to certain laws or processes should not call into question a person's commitment to opposing slavery.

75 - Should trafficking victims ever be jailed?

This topic draws criticism but reflects the potential disparity be-tween theory and practice in the response to human trafficking. It also illustrates how beliefs can change within the anti-trafficking community and how challenging it can be to promote an evolu-tion of our thinking.

Of course, *victims of crime should never be jailed*. We've examined the necessity of both a victim-centered and a trauma-informed response, so we understand we never wish to re-victimize or re-traumatize victims. But the topic of placing a trafficking victim in jail has been part of the conversation since the earliest days of the TVPA because sometimes trafficking victims may also be considered offenders (as described in Chapter 1, Question 11). A woman who could be arrested for prostitution but whom we believe to actually be a victim of trafficking provides just one ex-ample. The question of jailing a victim also arises when discussing juvenile victim-offenders, especially if the victim is a runaway or otherwise at-risk.

The debate over the temporary jailing of victims also results from real-world limitations on victim housing and from a desire to break the cycle of violence between trafficker and victim. Let me explain.

Suppose a police department—part of a multisector human trafficking task force—conducts an operation (*operation* is a better word than *raid*) against a brothel and a group of women are found working there. As workers in the brothel, they live in the brothel, where they are controlled by the brothel owner. Per-haps these women speak little or no English and are not familiar with the area. The task force must decide how best to protect the women.

In an ideal case, a shelter would be available to handle all the needs of the victims. But remember that victims are free to walk away, and their trafficker may have instilled such fear that they will walk away from the shelter and return to the trafficker or their associates. But if no shelter is available, where do the women go? Out on the street? Or back to the brothel?

Treating these women as offenders allows police to jail them, at least for the short term of 24 hours. If nothing else, the cycle of violence is briefly broken, and the women can rest, eat, and shower. They can have access to human trafficking advocates who can assist them.

These offenders can be released, "un-arrested," if you will, by police at any time. Depending upon the circumstances and the policies of the prosecutor, the person's arrest record may show the person was arrested but no charges were filed. In some states, a conviction of prostitution can be vacated by the court if the person convicted was determined to be a victim of trafficking and forced into prostitution.

A juvenile victim-offender can present the same challenges. Is the minor placed in the custody of juvenile probation or juvenile hall, or does the juvenile walk away, most likely to the trafficker they depend upon for food, shelter, and affection? If a shelter exists, an additional consideration arises when placing at-risk children with other at-risk children: Is there a possibility one child will recruit or befriend other children, perhaps leading to their trafficking victimization? (Laws regarding juveniles and their arrest and protective custody options can vary between jurisdictions.)

The difficult realities of housing and protecting victims in these types of situations run head-on into the desire to treat victims *as victims*.

What matters most is how police, juvenile probation officers, prosecutors, and victim service providers each view the victim and how they work together to best care for the victim. A victim-offender treated with respect, offered assistance in ways that reflect an understanding the offender has also been victimized, and eventually treated solely as a victim may have a better chance of being removed from an ongoing cycle of violence.

In the early days of the TVPA nobody attempting to embrace the philosophy of a victim-centered and trauma-informed response would even hint at approval of short-term incarceration of a victim-offender. Today, that attitude has begun to change. There are victim service providers who believe the best way to break the cycle of violence for victims is to place them in a locked facility *for a short period of time.* Some very experienced anti-trafficking experts who work closely with victims support this practice when necessary. A few occasionally make their stance public, but others prefer to keep their opinions quiet for fear of conflict with colleagues. Often, they simply do not protest when those they serve are temporarily jailed.

These dilemmas often result from a lack of human trafficking shelters, but the lack of a shelter is not the only reason. Only when we understand how deeply traffickers can coerce and manipulate their victims and how traffickers can retain control even when their victims are safe in police and service-provider hands do we begin to comprehend how difficult it is to identify victims and keep them safe.

This discussion will continue among those involved in assisting victims. We all know what we would like to happen in a perfect world. Alas, our world is not perfect.

76 - What was the impact of shutting down the Craigslist Adult Services section?

In September 2010, the online advertising site Craigslist closed their Adult Services section as a result of a campaign led by over a dozen state attorney generals. The adult section of Craigslist contained subtly disguised ads for commercial sex, some of which involved force, fraud, or coercion, or involved minors; both of these circumstances constitute human trafficking. The closure of the adult section was deemed a victory by many abolitionists, but was the impact more symbolic than practical?

The elimination of the adult section was limited only to Craigslist advertising within the United States. Craigslist hosts advertising sites around the world, so the impact on sex trafficking (and the loss of Craigslist revenue) was limited to the United States.

When advertisers could no longer post ads to Craigslist, they moved elsewhere to sites like Backpage.com, which provide the same type of advertising platform. Or they moved to private hosting sites where members pay a fee for access to ads and sometimes have the option to post "reviews" of the services purchased. (One infamous site, MyRedBook.com, was shut down after a federal investigation.) In any case, there is little evidence that shutting down the Craigslist section had any significant impact on trafficking.

Another aspect of this topic, the relationship between law enforcement agencies and advertising sites, merits discussion. Many law enforcement officers involved in anti-trafficking investigations did not support the closure of the Craigslist section because in their experience, Craigslist quickly and reliably released information to law enforcement agencies when sex trafficking was being investigated. This type of information sharing is not always possible with private (or "underground") advertising sites. Often (but not always) law enforcement investigators believe it is easier to investigate trafficking cases with cooperative companies, and one major advertising site hosting ads in their jurisdiction is easier to monitor than several smaller online sites. This same argument is now voiced whenever the discussion of shutting down the adult section of Backpage.com arises.

As of July 2015, a new tactic is being employed against Backpage.com. Major credit card companies including American Express, MasterCard, and Visa have announced they will no longer allow their credit cards to be used when purchasing advertising on Backpage.com. But those using Backpage.com to advertise commercial sex are already adapting to this change. Only time will tell whether this policy change by the credit card companies will have any real impact.

So what exactly did shutting down the Craigslist section accomplish?

This action did raise awareness of how online advertising provides the critical link between the seller and buyer of commercial sex and how sex trafficking victims can be exploited in this environment. Also, consumers who use the free posting sections in Craigslist to sell and buy items and services not related to commercial sex were exposed to how these types of companies receive a large portion of their revenue, potentially giving these consumers a reason to go elsewhere. Finally, shutting down the Adult Services section in Craigslist provided an opportunity for individuals and organizations to take a visible stand against human trafficking.

Not all anti-trafficking initiatives actually reduce human trafficking, nor are they always intended to. Analyzing the potential consequences and looking for unforeseen consequences are both critical steps when exploring potential anti-trafficking actions. Some efforts raise public awareness; others improve the response of law enforcement or service providers. And some efforts arise from the simple moral ground that requires us to act if we oppose slavery. But, however worthy these aspirations, they do not guarantee our efforts will always have a tangible outcome.

CHAPTER 8

Human Trafficking: Final Questions

I end with two final questions. The first is a good bit of trivia for an abolitionist to know. The second is a deeply personal question, yet one I am routinely asked.

77 - Who was William Wilberforce?

William Wilberforce (1759–1833) was an English politician and leading abolitionist of his time. He was instrumental in the passage of the Slave Trade Act of 1807, which abolished slavery within the British Empire.

People ask this question because his name is included in the TVPRA title, *William Wilberforce Trafficking Victims Protection Reauthorization Act of 2008*.[1] When his name was included in the title, many people had to ask, "Who is William Wilberforce?" So now you know.

Wilberforce was also involved in the creation of the Society for the Prevention of Cruelty to Animals (SPCA). The 2006 movie, *Amazing Grace*, tells the story of Wilberforce's abolitionist efforts.

78 - What is the most heinous human trafficking crime I've seen?

I end with this question because, as explained in the preface, my intent is to address the questions about human trafficking and modern slavery I am most commonly asked. And believe it or not, this is one of them.

Frankly, I find the question curious. I'm rarely asked to describe the most heinous or ugliest thing I saw as a patrol officer or sex crimes investigator. (I saw many things I hope to one day forget.)

I believe people are comfortable asking me this question because they hope it will help them understand what slavery looks like in the 21ˢᵗ century. They inherently realize the images used to promote awareness of human trafficking are simplistic. They seek an image of the reality of modern slavery to help them understand. Their knowledge of slavery is most likely limited to the context of the Civil War when slavery was—literally and figuratively—black and white. It was so much easier to see and—though repugnant—comprehend. In the same respect, the response to slavery at that time seemed simple: emancipate slaves, and later ratify the 13ᵗʰ Amendment to our Constitution.

But this new slavery, human trafficking, is so very much more complex, and the response to it even more so. I hope you now appreciate this reality along with the challenges we face in the future.

In any case, answering this question offers no real value, so I leave it unanswered. Hopefully, my contributors and I have provided a glimpse into the dark corners of our world where human beings lack freedom, where they are exploited through their toil and abused by many, and where they dream that one day someone will help them and—they will be free.

If we desire an image to cling to, let it be an image of those who oppose slavery, those who seek justice and who daily respond to the challenges involved in assisting victims and imprisoning traffickers. Let that image be an abolitionist!

You may choose to look the other way
but you can never say again that you did not know.
WILLIAM WILBERFORCE

ABOUT THE AUTHOR

John Vanek is a consultant and speaker focusing on human trafficking and the collaborative response to modern slavery. He has worked with the United States Department of Justice, the Office of the United States Attorneys, California's Office of the Attorney General, California POST, the California District Attorneys Association, the National Law Enforcement Training Network, the Not For Sale Campaign, the Freedom Network Training Institute, and other governmental and private organizations. John is an adjunct professor in the Graduate School of International Policy & Management at the Middlebury Institute of International Studies at Monterey.

John retired in the rank of lieutenant from the San Jose Police Department, where he managed the San Jose Police Human Trafficking Task Force, and holds an M.A. in Leadership from Saint Mary's College of California.

To contact John or see more of his writing on human trafficking, collaboration, and leadership visit: www.johnvanek.com

For updates on topics addressed in *The Essential Abolitionist*, useful links, and anti-trafficking job openings, visit:

https://www.facebook.com/theessentialabolitionist

Follow John on Twitter: @JohnJVanek

ACKNOWLEDGMENTS

This book is the result of a decade engaged in the response to human trafficking and would not have been possible without the support, encouragement, and passion of many people. The earliest support came from San Jose Police Chief Rob Davis and Deputy Chief Dave Cavallaro, both now retired. In 2006, when few understood the importance of responding to human trafficking and the BJA/OVC Human Trafficking Task Force program was in its infancy, Rob and Dave gave me their complete support to pursue the creation of the task force. Collaboration is always easier when your agency's leadership supports and endorses your effort. At the time, I never imagined where the path would lead me.

In 2006 the nascent South Bay Coalition to End Human Trafficking was the umbrella organization bringing anti-trafficking activists together, including victim services providers, investigators, prosecutors, and community activists. Together we struggled to not only create a response but also to learn the *how-to* of creating and implementing that response. Both aspects were challenging but rewarding. Much of what I share with others today about collaboration is a result of our early efforts. I am immensely grateful to have had the opportunity to work with everyone connected to the Coalition. Many of my colleagues cannot be named for security reasons, so a list would be incomplete. To every Coalition member, please know your service to others is inspiring, and I miss working with you.

ACKNOWLEDGMENTS

San Jose Police Officer Jennifer Dotzler was the first investigator assigned to the task force full-time, bringing impeccable investigative skills, a keen sense of humor, and professionalism to the newly-created position. Thank you for everything.

I've been extremely fortunate to cross paths with many abolitionists, colleagues, and clients who have helped inform my work and this book. Perhaps the most profound aspect of anti-trafficking work is that abolitionists come from every point on the political spectrum and cross every social divide to fight slavery. Thank you all.

I greatly appreciate the guest contributors included in *The Essential Abolitionist*. The scope of this book is wider and deeper because of their insights. Each expert invited to contribute to this book jumped at the opportunity with an enthusiastic "Yes!" Their subject matter expertise helps readers gain better insight into the complexities of human trafficking, and their spirit of collaboration embodies the very principles this book promotes. This book was strengthened immensely by their involvement.

The Essential Abolitionist would not have been published without the support of many dedicated abolitionists who supported *The Essential Abolitionist* Kickstarter project, including Alabaster Jar Project, whose donation was supported by a donor who wishes to remain anonymous; the Bay Area Anti-Trafficking Coalition (BAATC); Mary Benson, a community activist; Doug and Sheri Blackwell; Lorenzo Duenas, Santa Rosa Junior College District Police Department; Kirsten Foot; the Fritz family; Kathy Jackson; Antonia Lavine; Jim and Mara McMahon, McMahon & Associates; Marc D. Remington; Richard and Gail Siebert; and Christopher J. Warren, Founder, First Responder One.

Several people cast a critical eye over the manuscript, including my content editors Professor Kirsten Foot, Benjamin Greer, Esq., and Deputy Chief (Ret.) Derek Marsh. Your combined experience, expertise, and passion for bringing clarity to complexity grace every page. Kelly Johnson proofread the manuscript catching things previously missed. Any remaining errors are my responsibility.

My editor, Kate Cunningham, was indispensable. Not only did she bring her word-smithing prowess to this project, she adopted for herself my vision of helping others understand the challenges in the response to human trafficking. Without previous experience on the topic, Kate brought the perspective of someone learning about these challenges for the first time. As a result, the book is much stronger.

Gil Zamora and I worked together on several projects while we were both with the San Jose Police Department, including many graphic art projects supporting our human trafficking task force. Now retired, Gil is nationally-recognized as a forensic artist and instructor on the art and discipline of Cognitive Sketch. He is a masterful collaborator, and I am thrilled Gil agreed to design the cover of *The Essential Abolitionist*. You can learn more about Gil's work at www.zamorasketch.com.

Over the past decade close personal friends have politely allowed me to ramble on for hours about modern slavery while offering their encouragement and support. The coffee was always good. Thank you.

My son, Ian, and his wife, Michelle, are great supporters. I'm proud you both serve others in your professions.

Finally, I owe my greatest appreciation to my wife, Dawn, who has supported my passions and given me the freedom to pursue them. Dawn is my greatest collaborator, and the most compassionate person I've ever met. I love you.

CONTRIBUTOR BIOGRAPHIES

Alejandra Acevedo, Esq., is currently a Human Trafficking Training and Technical Assistance Specialist for the Office for Victims of Crime Training and Technical Assistance Center (OVC TTAC). In this position, she responds to the human trafficking related training and technical assistance needs of the OVC grantees, victim service providers, law enforcement, and other affiliated professionals. Prior to joining OVC TTAC, Alejandra was the Policy and Publications Specialist for the U.S. Department of State Office to Monitor and Combat Trafficking in Persons in the Reports and Political Affairs section, where she managed the publication of the Trafficking in Persons Report and conducted extensive research on human trafficking issues in countries around the world and relevant governments' efforts to confront it. As a law clerk for National District Attorneys Association, National Center for Prosecution of Child Abuse, she researched and synthesized research, case law, and state and federal statutes on child abuse and served as a subject matter expert on domestic child trafficking. Alejandra also served as a legal intern and board member for Save the Young Organization (SAYO) where she administered seminars on Human Rights, Domestic Violence, and Child Trafficking in rural Kumbo, Cameroon. Alejandra holds a Bachelor of Arts degree in Political Science, certificate in International Relations, and minor in Mass Communications from the University of Florida. She also holds a juris doctorate from the Washington College of Law, American University.

Jon A. Daggy is a Detective Sergeant with the Indianapolis Metropolitan Police Department. Jon grew up in Mishawaka, Indiana and joined the department in 1989. Since 2005, he has been a detective and supervisor in the Human Trafficking Vice Unit. He is a court expert on the subjects of human trafficking investigations and transnational organized crime. Jon speaks regularly on human trafficking, has trained law enforcement officers in human trafficking and vice investigations, and holds a Bachelor of Science degree in Criminal Justice from Ball State University.

Melissa Farley is a psychologist and Executive Director of Prostitution Research & Education. Melissa has 49 publications in the field of violence against women, most of which address prostitution, pornography, and sex trafficking. Her work, with many co-authors, has been used by governments in South Africa, Canada, New Zealand, Ghana, United Kingdom, Cambodia, and the United States for education and policy development. In the last decade Melissa has begun studying sex buyers, resulting in the 2015 publication of an article showing that sex buyers have many of the same attitudes and sexually coercive behaviors of highly sexually aggressive men.

Susan French was Senior Special Counsel for Human Trafficking in the Human Trafficking Prosecution Unit, Criminal Section, Civil Rights Division, U.S. Department of Justice, where she investigated and prosecuted labor and sex human trafficking cases on behalf of the United States throughout the 50 states, territories, and possessions. Susan recently was the Senior Staff Attorney for the Anti-Trafficking Project, International Human Rights Clinic, George Washington University Law School in Washington DC. Susan has and continues to consult and train national and international law enforcement and civil society organizations.

Dr. Annie Isabel Fukushima is an Assistant Professor with the Ethnic Studies Program and the College of Social Work at the University of Utah. Prior to joining the faculty at University of Utah, she received her Ph.D. from University of California, Berkeley in Ethnic Studies with a Designated Emphasis in Women, Gender and Sexuality Studies and was an Andrew W. Mellon Postdoctoral Fellow at Rutgers University (2013–2015). In 2015 she was recognized by the National Center for Institutional Diversity (NCID) as an Exemplary Diversity Scholar. Dr. Fukushima's scholarly and public works on immigration, citizenship, victimhood, criminality, and violence has appeared in multiple edited anthologies, encyclopedias, and handbooks for ABC-Clio, Greenwood Press, and MacMillan, scholarly peer reviewed articles in journals such as *Feminist Formations, Frontiers: Journal of Womens Studies,* and *Praxis: Gender & Cultural Critiques* and non-scholarly publications in *The Nation, Foreign Policy in Focus, Alternet,* and *Asia Times Online.* Currently she is a co-editor for Third Woman Press, a Queer and Feminist of Color publisher, and their inaugural anthology being co-edited with Dr. Fukushima, Dr. Layli Maparyan, Dr. Anita Revilla, and Dr. Matt Richardson. Her teaching experiences encompass a wide range of institutions: She has taught in community college (Laney College), in liberal arts colleges (Scripps College), at state institutions (San Francisco State University), and at research universities (University of California, Berkeley; University of California, Santa Cruz; Rutgers University; and University of Utah). She has served as an expert witness and consultant regarding human trafficking. She has worked at all levels of organizations.

Benjamin Thomas Greer is currently the Senior Executive on Legal Issues for the Paragon Team. The Paragon Team's mission is to help governments advance their anti-trafficking response through law enforcement training and intelligence gathering specifically designed to improve their Tier ranking with the United States Department of State's annual TIP report. He is a Former Special Deputy Attorney General—Human Trafficking Special Projects Team for the California Department of Justice—Office of the Attorney General; former research attorney for the California District Attorneys Association (CDAA); and Legal and

Legislative Consultant for the Coalition to Abolish Slavery & Trafficking (CAST).

Sarah Jakiel is the Chief Programs Officer of Polaris. She sits on the Executive Management Team responsible for the overall operation of the organization and helps to support Polaris' programs. She has been on the leading edge of anti-human trafficking efforts both domestically and globally since 2005. Sarah started with Polaris, launching and directing the National Human Trafficking Resource Center and filling a critical service in the anti-trafficking field focused on victim identification, helping survivors access help, and directing key intelligence to law enforcement to fight traffickers. She speaks and trains frequently on topics ranging from engaging technology in the fight against human trafficking to the development and implementation of human trafficking hotlines as the core of a successful national anti-trafficking strategy. Sarah currently advises other countries on local, national and regional efforts to develop effective anti-trafficking response mechanisms. Sarah holds Bachelor of Arts degrees in Political Science and French from the University of Virginia. After living abroad for several years in Eastern Europe and Southeast Asia where Sarah observed human trafficking firsthand, she returned to the U.S. and pursued an MA in Ethics, Peace, and Global Affairs from American University where she focused her graduate research on both transnational and domestic human trafficking.

Cindy C. Liou, Esq. is a consultant, trainer, author, and attorney who practices law in the areas of human trafficking, immigration law, family law, and domestic violence. Recently, she was the Director of the Human Trafficking Project at Asian Pacific Islander Legal Outreach and the Co-Chair of the Policy Committee of the Freedom Network to Empower Trafficked and Enslaved Persons (USA). She is the winner of the 2013 San Francisco Collaborative Against Human Trafficking Modern Day Abolitionist Award for Policy and Advocacy. Cindy is also the coauthor of several articles and the second edition of *Representing Survivors of Human Trafficking*.

Derek Marsh retired in the rank of Deputy Chief from the Westminster (CA) Police Department after more than 26 years of service in 2013. In 2004, Derek helped launch the Orange County Human Trafficking Task Force. He served as the co-chair of the OCHTTF from 2004-2012, during which time he developed and taught four courses in human trafficking across the state of California, assisted in creating three human trafficking training DVDs, wrote multiple grants, and twice provided expert witness testimony on human trafficking to Congress. He has presented anti-trafficking trainings across California and the United States, and in Saipan, Italy, and Argentina. He teaches a course on human trafficking at Vanguard University, in Costa Mesa, CA. Derek holds a Master of Arts in Human Behavior, a Master of Public Administration, and graduated from FBI National Academy, Class #224. Currently, Derek is the Bureau of Justice Assistance Visiting Fellow in Human Trafficking, which involves researching, developing and providing training and technical support for human trafficking task forces across the United States.

Shamere McKenzie is the CEO of the Sun Gate Foundation, an anti-trafficking organization that provides educational opportunities for victims of human trafficking. Turning her past adversities as a victim of domestic sex trafficking into engagement, Shamere has become an activist in the fight against human trafficking, bringing about social and political change in America and around the world. She serves on the speaker's bureau for the Fredrick Douglas Family Initiative and Survivors of Slavery organizations and holds a Bachelor of Science degree in Criminology and Criminal Justice from Loyola University Chicago.

Nicole Moler is the Director of the National Human Trafficking Resource Center (NHTRC), the national, 24/7, confidential, anti-trafficking hotline and resource center serving victims and survivors of human trafficking and the anti-trafficking community in the United States. Nicole joined Polaris in 2007 as part of the team that designed, launched, and operated the NHTRC with the goal of providing human trafficking victims and survivors with access to critical support and services to get help and stay safe and equipping the anti-trafficking community with the tools to effectively combat all forms of human trafficking. Nicole also helped to develop and directs the BeFree Textline which was launched in 2013 as a means of increasing access to victims and survivors and at-risk populations through the use of an SMS text-based hotline. Nicole has provided training and technical assistance to other countries on the development, implementation, and operation of human trafficking hotlines. Nicole has a Master of Arts in International Affairs with a concentration in Conflict and Conflict Resolution from the George Washington University.

Sandra Morgan, PhD, RN, directs the Global Center for Women and Justice at Vanguard University of Southern California. Drawing on her experience as a pediatric nurse, pastor's wife, administrator of the Orange County Human Trafficking Task Force, and professor, Sandra has developed valuable insights into community engagement. She is co-host of the *Ending Human Trafficking* podcast with listeners in more than fifty countries. The U.S. Clearinghouse for the Administration of Youth and Family Services recommends the podcast (http://www.vanguard.edu/gcwj/) as a way to get up to speed on human trafficking issues.

Lynette M. Parker, Esq., is clinical faculty (Immigration Practice Area) at the Alexander Community Law Center, Santa Clara University School of Law since March 2000, where she also teaches, and provides technical assistance on U visa and T visa cases. She has co-authored *Representing Survivors of Human Trafficking: A Promising Practices Handbook*, 1st edition 2010 and 2nd edition 2014, Immigrant Legal Resource Center (ILRC). Lynette has been a member of the Executive Committee of the South Bay Coalition to End Human Trafficking since 2005 and a commission member of the Santa Clara County Human Trafficking Commission since 2014.

Stephanie Kay Richard, Esq., is the Policy & Legal Services Director at the Coalition to Abolish Slavery & Trafficking (CAST) where she provides direct legal services to survivors of human trafficking and technical consultation on human trafficking cases nationwide. She has been involved in the anti-trafficking movement for over 10 years. During this time she has served as the domestic lead for the Alliance to End Slavery & Trafficking (ATEST) and the policy Co-Chair of the Freedom Network, USA, two national U.S.-based coalitions working to improve federal and state laws and the implementation of these laws to better serve trafficking survivors in the United States. Stephanie graduated summa cum laude from American University, Washington College of Law, where she was the recipient of a public interest/ public service scholarship. She is licensed to practice law in California, Maryland, Minnesota, and Washington, D.C.

Kiricka Yarbough Smith serves as the Chair of the North Carolina Coalition Against Human Trafficking (NCCAHT) and consults with the North Carolina Council for Women's Human Trafficking Project. Kiricka is an investigator on the University of North Carolina, School of Social Work's project addressing child trafficking in the welfare system and serves as faculty for the Futures Without Violence project on building collaboration to address human trafficking in domestic violence and sexual assault cases, funded by the U.S. Department of Justice's Office on Violence Against Women. Kiricka has served as a consultant with the North Carolina Conference of District Attorneys to provide regional trainings on human trafficking to law enforcement and prosecutors and has provided training and technical assistance to service providers, including resources and referrals for survivors of human trafficking.

Mark Wexler is co-founder and executive director of the global anti-slavery organization Not For Sale and co-founder and partner of Just Business, an international investment group that accelerates social enterprises. The two entities co-created the beverage company REBBL. He also started the San Francisco-based Invention Hub, a business incubator and co-working space. Mark manages Not For Sale's senior staff, operationalizes strategic relationships with partner institutions, and helps steer overall organizational direction. He is currently a lecturer at the University of California Berkeley Extension's Entrepreneurship and Innovation program.

RESOURCES & WEBSITES

New sources of information related to human trafficking and response efforts appear monthly. Some resources, though several years old, are still valuable for their examination of human trafficking and the dilemmas faced in anti-trafficking efforts. This short list (in addition to the sources included in the Notes) is intended to provide readers with options to further their knowledge and understanding of this topic. New resources of potential value to readers of *The Essential Abolitionist* are posted at:

https://www.facebook.com/theessentialabolitionist

Books on Human Trafficking

Bales, K, & Soodalter, R, (2009). *The slave next door: Human trafficking and slavery in America today.* Berkeley: University of California Press.

Batstone, D. (2007). *Not for sale: The return of the global slave trade—and how we can fight it.* New York: Harper Collins Publishers.

Farley, M. (2007) *Prostitution and trafficking in Nevada: Making the connections.* San Francisco: Prostitution Research & Education.

Foot, K. (2015). *Collaborating against human trafficking: Cross-sector challenges and practices.* Lanham: Rowman & Littlefield Publishers.

Lloyd, R. (2011). *Girls like us: Fighting for a world where girls are not for sale, an activist finds her calling and heals herself.* New York: Harper Collins Publishers.

Skinner, E. B. (2008). *A crime so monstrous: Face-to-face with modern-day slavery.* New York: Free Press.

Publications Available Online

Human Trafficking Task Force e-Guide: www.ovcttac.gov/taskforceguide/eguide/

Police Chief Magazine. July 2014. (This issue contains several articles related to human trafficking valuable to local law enforcement agencies and is available at www.policechiefmagazine.org.)

Stop Enslavement. Stop Trafficking!: Anti-Human Trafficking Newsletter. (This free monthly newsletter provides timely news on recent developments, available at http:www.stopenslavement.org.)

United Nations. *Protocol to prevent, suppress and punish trafficking in persons especially women and children.* (2004). Supplement to the United Nations Convention against Transnational Organized Crime. Referred to as "The Palermo Protocol," this international protocol is similar to the TVPA. (http://www.unodc.org/documents/treaties/UNTOC/Publications/TOC%20Convention/TOCebook-e.pdf)

United Nations Office on Drugs and Crime. Global report on trafficking in persons. (2014). (http://www.unodc.org/documents/data-and-analysis/glotip/GLOTIP_2014_full_report.pdf)

U.S. Department of State. *Trafficking in persons report.* (2015). (http:www.state.gov/j/tip/rls/tiprpt/)

Websites

Blue Campaign, U.S. Department of Homeland Security: www. dhs.gov/blue-campaign

Coalition to Abolish Slavery & Trafficking (CAST): www.castla. org

ECPAT USA: http://www.ecpatusa.org/home

Florida Coalition Against Human Trafficking: http://www. stophumantrafficking.org/

Freedom Network: http://freedomnetworkusa.org/

Free the Slaves: http://www.freetheslaves.net/

National Center for Missing and Exploited Children: http:// www.missingkids.com/home

Office to Monitor and Combat Trafficking in Persons, U.S. Department of State: www.state.gov/j/tip/

Polaris Project: http://www.polarisproject.org

Prostitution Research & Education: http://prostitutionresearch. com/

United Nations Global Initiative to Fight Human Trafficking: http://www.ungift.org/

U.S. Catholic Sisters Against Trafficking: http://www. sistersagainsttrafficking.org/

ENDNOTES

Chapter 1: Human Trafficking: Basic Definitions and Terms

1 Victims of Trafficking and Violence Protection Act of 2000, Public Law 106-383, 106th Cong. (2000). Available from U.S. State Department: http://www.state.gov/documents/organization/10492.pdf

2 Trafficking Victims Protection, U.S. Code Chapter 78, § 7102. (2000). Available from Cornell University Law School: https://www.law.cornell.edu/uscode/text/22/7102

3 Kaplan, E. (2005). *Child soldiers around the world.* Available at http://www.cfr.org/human-rights/child-soldiers-around-world/p9331

4 TVPA (2000).

5 TVPA (2000).

6 Foot, K., & Vanek, J. (2012). Toward constructive engagement between local law enforcement and mobilization and advocacy nongovernmental organizations about human trafficking: Recommendations for law enforcement executives. *Law Enforcement Executive Forum, 12*(1). Available at http://faculty.washington.edu/kfoot/Publications/EFJ%2012.1%20Foot-Vanek.pdf

7 http://californiaagainstslavery.org/

Chapter 2: Modern Slavery: Traffickers and Victims

1 International Labour Organization. (2012). *ILO 2012 Global estimate of forced labor, Executive summary.* Available at http://www.ilo.org/wcmsp5/groups/public/---ed_norm/---declaration/documents/publication/wcms_181953.pdf

2 Bales, K. (1999). *Disposable people: New slavery in the global economy.* Berkeley: University of California Press.

3 Free the Slaves. (2015). Slavery Today. Retrieved on November 9, 2015 from http://www.freetheslaves.net/about-slavery/slavery-today/

4 Kara, S. (2009). *Sex trafficking: Inside the business of modern slavery.* New York: Columbia University Press.

5 U.S. Department of Justice, Office of Justice Programs, Bureau of Justice Statistics. (2011). *Characteristics of suspected human trafficking incidents, 2008-2010.* Available at http://www.bjs.gov/content/pub/pdf/cshti0810.pdf

6 Estes, R.J., & Weiner, N.A. (2001). *The commercial sexual exploitation of children in the U.S., Canada and Mexico.* Philadelphia: University of Pennsylvania. Available at http://www.thenightministry.org/070_facts_figures/030_research_links/060_homeless_youth/CommercialSexualExploitationofChildren.pdf

7 Finkelhor, D., & Stransky, M. (2008). *How many juveniles are involved in prostitution in the U.S.?* (Fact Sheet). Available at http://www.unh.edu/ccrc/prostitution/Juvenile_Prostitution_factsheet.pdf

8 Institute of Medicine and National Research Council of the National Academies. (2013). *Confronting commercial sexual exploitation and sex trafficking of minors in the United States.* Available at https://iom.nationalacademies.org/~/media/Files/Report%20Files/2013/Sexual-Exploitation-Sex-Trafficking/sextraffickingminors_rb.pdf

9 U.S. Departments of Justice, Health and Human Services, and Homeland Security. (2013). *Federal strategic action plan on services for victims of human trafficking in the United States 2013-2017.* Available at http://www.ovc.gov/pubs/FederalHumanTraffickingStrategicPlan.pdf

10 U.S. Department of Justice, Federal Bureau of Investigation. (2015). *Crime in the United States 2014.* Available at https://www.fbi.gov/about-us/cjis/ucr/crime-in-the-u.s/2014/crime-in-the-u.s.-2014

11 *ILO 2012 Global estimate of forced labor.*

12 *ILO 2012 Global estimate of forced labor.*

13 United Nations Office on Drugs and Crime. *Transnational organized crime: Let's put them out of business.* Available at https://www.unodc.org/toc/en/crimes/organized-crime.html

14 International Labour Organization. (2014). *Profits and poverty: The economics of forced labour.* Available at http://www.ilo.org/global/publications/ilo-bookstore/order-online/books/WCMS_243391/lang--en/index.htm

15 Free the Slaves. (2015).

16 Skinner, E. B. (2008). *A crime so monstrous: Face-to-face with modern-day slavery.* New York: Free Press.

17 Polaris Project. National Human Trafficking Resource Center (NHTRC) Annual Report, 1/1/2014–12/31/2014. Available at http://www.traffickingresourcecenter.org/sites/default/files/2014%20NHTRC%20Annual%20Report_Final

18 Federal Bureau of Investigation. (2014). 168 juveniles recovered in nationwide operation targeting commercial child sex trafficking [Press release]. Available at https://www.fbi.gov/news/pressrel/press-releases/168-juveniles-recovered-in-nationwide-operation-targeting-commercial-child-sex-trafficking

19 U.S. Department of Justice. (2009). Wisconsin couple sentenced for forcing a woman to work as their domestic servant for 19 years [Press release]. Available at http://www.justice.gov/opa/pr/wisconsin-couple-sentenced-forcing-woman-work-their-domestic-servant-19-years

20 U.S. Department of Justice. (2010). California woman sentenced to five years imprisonment for forced labor of domestic servant [Press release]. Available http://www.state.gov/m/ds/rls/140326.htm

21 U.S. Department of Justice. (2009). Five sentenced for forcing Guatemalan girls and women to work as prostitutes in Los Angeles [Press release]. Available at http://www.justice.gov/opa/pr/five-sentenced-forcing-guatemalan-girls-and-women-work-prostitutes-los-angeles

22 Ted Talks (Producer). (2010, March 29). Kevin Bales: How to combat modern slavery [Video file]. Available at: https://www.youtube.com/watch?v=HUM2rCIUdeI

23 Robinson, R. (2011, July 21). Undocumented women servicing field workers, streetwalkers in seeding motels, high-end flesh sold at high-end events: Sex sells in Monterey County. *Monterey County Weekly*. Available at: http://www.montereycountyweekly.com/news/cover/undocumented-women-servicing-field-workers-streetwalkers-in-seedy-motels-high/article_f16d4c7d-bb82-5835-a504-a63928bc2884.html

Chapter 3: Responding to Human Trafficking: Concepts and Resources

1 Gallagher, A.T. (2002). Trafficking, smuggling and human rights: tricks and treaties. *Forced Migration Review, 12,* 25-28.

2 Jordan, A.D. (2002, March). Human rights or wrongs? The struggle for a rights-based response to trafficking in human beings. *Gender and Development, 10*(1), 28-37. [Special Issue: Trafficking and Slavery].

3 Hua, J. (2011). *Trafficking women's human rights.* Minneapolis: University of Minnesota Press.

4 Chevrette, R., Keating, C., Koblitz, A. H., Kuo, K., Lee, C. T., & Switzer, H. (Eds.). (2015). Anti-violence iconographies of the cage: Diasporan crossings and the (un)tethering of subjectivities. *Frontiers: A Journal of Women's Studies,* [Special Issue "Transnational Feminisms"].

5 Brennan, D. (2014). *Life interrupted: trafficking into forced labor in the United States.* Durham: Duke University Press.

6 See the work of Niamh Reilly. *Women's human rights: Seeking gender justice in a globalising age.* Palgrave, 2009.

7 Foot, K. (2016). *Collaborating against human trafficking: Cross-sector challenges and practices.* Lanham: Rowman & Littlefield.

8 Office to Monitor and Combat Trafficking in Persons. (2011). *About Us.* Retrieved on October 11, 2015 from http://www.state.gov/j/tip/about/index.htm

9 Ibid.

10 United Nations Office on Drugs and Crime. Protocol to prevent, suppress and punish trafficking in persons especially women and children. (2004) Available at http://www.unodc.org/documents/treaties/UNTOC/Publications/TOC%20Convention/TOCebook-e.pdf

11 Office to Monitor and Combat Trafficking in Persons. (2011). *About Us.* Retrieved on October 11, 2015 from http://www.state.gov/j/tip/about/index.htm

12 Ibid.

13 Ibid.

14 Ibid.

15 Ibid.

16 Ibid.

17 Ibid.

Chapter 4: Responding to Human Trafficking: Victims and Their Needs

1 U.S. Department of Justice, Office of Justice Programs. (2014). *Human trafficking task force e-Guide*. Available at https://www.ovcttac.gov/taskforceguide/eguide/1-understanding-human-trafficking/13-victim-centered-approach/

2 Wisconsin Office of Justice Assistance Violence Against Women Program Human Trafficking Protocol. (2012). 26.

Chapter 5: Responding to Human Trafficking: Law Enforcement Challenges

1 This analysis also would apply to state anti-trafficking and federal commercial sex trafficking violations.

2 I use "victim" not "survivor" because crimes have "victims."

3 18 U.S.C.§1589.

4 18 U.S.C. §1589 (c) (2).

5 U.S. Attorney's Office. (2011, April 18). Member and associates of Oceanside Crip street gangs and one hotel charged with racketeering conspiracy relating to prostitution of minors and adults and other crimes and criminal forfeiture [Press release]. Available at https://www.fbi.gov/sandiego/press-releases/2011/sd041811.htm

6 Typically, when examining how supply and demand factors influence labor trafficking, the subject is described as related to the "supply-chain" rather than as "demand reduction" even though these tactics seek to decrease demand. See Question 52 by Benjamin Thomas Greer.

7 Shively, M., Kliorys, K. (2012). *A national overview of prostitution and sex trafficking demand reduction efforts.* Abt Associates Inc.: Cambridge. Available at https://www.ncjrs.gov/pdffiles1/nij/grants/238796.pdf

Chapter 6: Be an Abolitionist: Your Role in Combating Human Trafficking

1 Others involved in the discussion of commercial sex trafficking and its connection to prostitution see the term "abolition" as referring to the abolition of prostitution. I view this use of the word as confined primarily to a specific academic sector.

2 Grace, A. & Lippert, S. (2014). Educating health care professionals on human trafficking. *Pediatric Emergency Care.* (12). Available at http://www.ncbi.nlm.nih.gov/pubmed/25407038

3 Levi Holtz, D., & Squatriglia, C. (2000, January 20). Berkeley landlord arrested in sex scheme / Police say he brought girls from India. *SFGate.* Available at http://www.sfgate.com/bayarea/article/Berkeley-Landlord-Arrested-in-Sex-Scheme-Police-2782509.php

4 International Labour Organization. (2012). *ILO 2012 Global estimate of forced labor, Executive summary.* Available at http://www.ilo.org/wcmsp5/groups/public/---ed_norm/---declaration/documents/publication/wcms_181953.pdf

5 Ibid.

6 Not for Sale. Annual report. (2014). Available at http://notforsalecampaign.org/impact/2014-annual-impact-report/

7 Polaris Project. Recognize the signs. Retrieved on November 18, 2015. Available at https://www.polarisproject.org/human-trafficking/recognizing-the-signs

Chapter 7: Human Trafficking: Myths & Misconceptions

1 Jervis, A. (2011, February 1). Child sex rings spike during Super Bowl week. *USA TODAY*. Available at http://usatoday30.usatoday.com/news/nation/2011-01-31-child-prostitution-super-bowl_N.htm

2 Roe-Sepowitz, D., & Gallagher, J. (2015). *Exploring the impact of the Super Bowl on sex trafficking*. Phoenix: Arizona State University School of Social Work. Available at https://www.mccaininstitute.org/programs/humanitarian-action/exploring-the-impact-of-the-super-bowl-on-sex-trafficking-2015

3 Queally, J. (2015, February 2). National sex trafficking sting nets nearly 600 arrests before Super Bowl. *Los Angeles Times*. Available at http://www.latimes.com/nation/nationnow/la-na-nn-sex-trafficking-sting-super-bowl-20150202-story.html

4 Mistrati, M., & Romano, R. (2010). *The dark side of chocolate* [Motion picture]. Denmark: Bastard Film & TV.

5 Farley, M. & Franzblau, K. (2014). *Online prostitution and trafficking*. Available at http://prostitutionresearch.com/2014/09/19/online-prostitution-and-trafficking/

6 Farley, M., Golding, J., Matthews, E.S., Malamuth, N., & Jarrett, L. (2015). Comparing sex buyers with men who do not buy sex: New data on prostitution and trafficking. *Journal of Interpersonal Violence* (August, 2015) 1-25. Available at http://prostitutionresearch.com/2015/09/01/men-who-buy-sex-have-much-in-common-with-sexually-coercive-men-new-study-shows-4/

7 Farley, M. & Franzblau, K. (2014). *Online prostitution and trafficking*. Available at http://prostitutionresearch.com/2014/09/19/online-prostitution-and-trafficking/

8 TVPA (2000).

9 Justice for Victims of Trafficking Act of 2015, S. 178, 114th Cong. (2015-2016). Available at https://www.congress.gov/bill/114th-congress/senate-bill/178

Chapter 8: Additional Questions about Human Trafficking

1 William Wilberforce Trafficking Victims Protection Reauthorization Act of 2008, H.R. 7311, 110th Cong. (2007-2009). Available at: http://www.state.gov/j/tip/laws/113178.htm

CPSIA information can be obtained
at www.ICGtesting.com
Printed in the USA
FSOW02n1825200116
15969FS